W9-BEV-488

ROCKING
THE CRADLE
CATHOLIC

RAISING LITTLE SAINTS IN A
LUKEWARM CULTURE

by
MARY MOORE

Unless otherwise noted, Scripture passages have been taken from the *Revised Standard Version*, Catholic edition. Copyright ©1946, 1952, 1971 by the Division of Christian Education of the National Council of the Churches of Christ in the USA. Used by permission. All rights reserved.

Quotes are taken from the English translation of the *Catechism of the Catholic Church* for the United States of America (indicated as CCC), 2nd ed. Copyright ©1997 by United States Catholic Conference – Libreria Editrice Vaticana.

©2009 Life Teen, Inc. All rights reserved. No part of this book, including interior design, cover design, and/or icons, may be reproduced or transmitted in any form, by any means (electronic, photocopying, recording, or otherwise) without prior written permission from the publisher.

The information contained herein is published and produced by Life Teen, Inc. The resources and practices are in full accordance with the Roman Catholic Church. The Life Teen® name and associated logos are trademarks registered with the United States Patent and Trademark Office. Use of the Life Teen® trademarks without prior permission is forbidden. Permission may be requested by contacting Life Teen, Inc. at 480-820-7001.

This book is dedicated to Tom and Marianne Phelan, the two best cradle Catholic rockers I know. Thank you for never compromising on your vocation to bring us up in the faith.

With special thanks to my tremendously supportive husband, Mark, who makes marriage seem like one big, long sleepover with my best friend.

And to my dearest Hannah, Ethan, and SaraBeth, who make this vocation of motherhood so rewarding.

ROCKING THE CRADLE CATHOLIC

introduction
WHERE IS NORTH?   *ix*

part 1
ON TRADITIONS & DAILY LIFE

ROCKING THE CRADLE CATHOLIC   *3*

THE BENEFITS OF HAVING CHILDREN   *7*

THE POWER OF DATING PARENTS   *11*

KEEPING WHOLLY THE SABBATH   *15*

AVOIDING THE RESOUNDING GONG   *19*

FINDING THE BETTER PART   *23*

AS FOR ME AND MY HOUSE   *27*

A RECIPE FOR RELATIONSHIP   *31*

part 2
ON SACRIFICE & OBEDIENCE

THE BLESSING OF LITTLE CROSSES   *37*

PACKAGE FOR A SOLDIER   *41*

OBEDIENCE: THE PATH TO TRUE FREEDOM?   *45*

TITHING 100% OBEDIENCE   *49*

FINDING YOUR SECONDARY MINISTRY   *53*

part 3
ON SACRAMENTS & THE LITURGICAL LIFE

PRUNING YOUR SPIRITUAL WEEDS   *59*

HOLD ON LOOSELY:
HOW A PARENT'S VOCATION CAN FOSTER A CHILD'S   *63*

THREE WORDS THAT WILL BRING YOU
CLOSER TO CHRIST   *67*

DECLUTTERING FOR THE RESURRECTION   *71*

CHOOSING A GODPARENT   *75*

MARRIAGE PREPARATION BEGINS SOONER
THAN YOU THINK   *79*

THE FRUITS OF AN ADVENT HEART   *83*

BRING ON THE HOLY FAMILY AT ADVENT   *87*

CREATING A SIMPLE ATMOSPHERE FOR
CHRIST AT ADVENT   *91*

....

part 4
WHERE IS MY HONORARY DEGREE?

....

RAISING A PRINCESS   *97*

THE GRACE OF PARENTAL HUMILITY   *101*

FINDING A ROLE MODEL   *105*

LEAVEN HELP US   *109*

RAISING PRO-LIFE KIDS   *113*

HAPPY CAMPERS   *117*

FOREWARD

Many a parent has uttered the questions: "Am I doing this right? Am I raising holy kids? Are our kids going to turn out ok? Will our children remain Catholic?" The role of parent does not come with a manual or annual performance reports. How do we as parents know if we are on track or not? In Rocking the Cradle Catholic you will get sound advice and inspirational insight into what an on-fire Catholic family looks like in today's culture. Through practical experiences, family activities, Scripture and Church traditions you will be given the tools to live more fully the call to be the "domestic church."

Life Teen is publishing this book for parents because parents are the primary catechists of their children. Catholic youth ministry is not just a "Teen Thing" but also a comprehensive approach to ministry that includes parents on the journey. We have found no better way to fulfill our mission of "leading teens closer to Christ" than by helping parents be holier themselves. The reality is that by families developing some simple and sacred times and practices, they will not just survive but thrive in our world today.

It can be a daunting task being a parent today, and for that reason we can be thankful for a book like this one and for guides like Mary Moore who is living the example each day. Take some time to read this book and discuss it with your spouse, your children or your Parent Life group – I believe it has the ability to truly transform the Domestic Church – your family!

Now get ready to be changed.

Randy Raus
Life Teen President / CEO

introduction

WHERE IS NORTH?

Let's just be honest with one another. Parenting in the modern world without a guide is a little like forging the high seas without a compass. Many a secular parenting authority claims to bear the right compass, yet to follow any one of them would have you going in a different direction than another. The truth is, no compass works without a True North. So too, parenting advice that isn't grounded in an understanding of our heavenly Father and his Word can't do much for parents when it comes to getting our kids to their ultimate destination: Heaven.

Don't get me wrong. Secular parenting advice can offer all sorts of gems when it comes to implementing a food pyramid or sleep training, but it lacks any kind of authority in counseling parents to shape their children's moral compasses. In fact, secular parenting experts, like most societal authorities, have fallen victim to the sweeping tide of moral relativism, and the sum of their advice is essentially the tenet *Whatever works for you is right.* Beyond choosing a child's birthday party theme or paint colors for the playroom, this parenting advice is hollow at best.

What about the big parenting questions for Catholics, like *How do I choose my child's godparent?* or *How can I encourage my child to go to Confession, be obedient for love's sake, or offer up little discomforts when it comes to chores?* And *How do I help them discern their vocation or discern my own ministry as a parent?*

Many of the answers to these questions, of course, are rooted in a parent who models obedience, sacrifice and regular participation in the sacraments – and who doesn't just talk about it. Beyond that, reflecting on God's Word and the riches of our Catholic faith can aid a parent in practicing their faith and can help them become more like the parent God wants you to be.

What I pray you find in this book is encouragement to do just that, *practice* your faith. Perfection in the faith, as perfection in parenting, is impossible. I have included several stories resulting in my own humility when I attempted both. May you be encouraged, and saved a struggle or two, by those stories.

The great news for Christian parents is that we have a Father in Heaven who adores us and who desires our eventual perfection in Him. He chose us to be the parents of our children, and as parents we can choose Love – the Person, not the nebulous idea - as our greatest tool. Along with a sense of humor and humility, love and obedience to Love go a long way in turning our ship North and getting our whole family to that great destination together.

My prayer is that the stories and reflections here will be a blessing to your family, and either in sympathy or empathy, you will find some of your own experiences here.

In the end, may we all find ourselves – humble and obedient - pointed North together as holy families.

QUESTIONS FOR CONTEMPLATION
& suggestions for action

These questions are meant to be used as an aid to help you grow closer to Christ in your journey as a parent and as a child of God. They can be used in a study group or on your own.

Each set of questions is broken into two sections, Contemplation and Action. Both sections should be used for self-reflection and growth. Often there is more than one suggestion in the Contemplation section. You need only choose one of these suggestions to follow, though you may choose more than one.

Occasionally, you will be asked to journal about your growth in faith. This is one of the greatest tools we have in our journey toward a relationship with God: the ability to dialogue with Him in writing regarding His work in our hearts. Some of the most powerful writings we have in the Church are from the personal journals and diaries of saints like Augustine, Therese of Lisieux and Maria Faustina Kowalska. Of course, your journal can remain entirely private. It is simply a way to reflect on God's continuing work on your heart and it can serve, at any time in your life, as a reminder of the many ways in which His incalculable love for you has manifested itself.

part 1

ON TRADITIONS & DAILY LIFE

ROCKING *the cradle catholic*

We have a little tradition in our family where my husband and I take each child out once a month on a date. It usually involves a simple formula: ice cream, lots of mom or dad's attention, and great conversation about what is going on in their life. On one date with my five year old daughter the topic turned toward college.

Since she was "graduating" from Kindergarten at the time, she was curious as to how many more "days of school" were left until she was grown up. I explained about the various stages of school and when I got to college, her interest piqued. Studying to be whatever she wanted interested her immensely, so she asked me the million dollar question that would reveal to me her goals for herself at the tender age of five.

"Can I go to school to be a princess?"

After gagging on my mint chip, I explained that a princess is a career into which a person is born and is fraught with much responsibility. She moved on to her second choice.

"I think I want to be a nun, but I'll have to see what their college looks like."

Far from being distraught that she hadn't chosen "Mommy" or "Teacher" or even "Freelance Writer," I was relieved. You see, it's entirely possible to meet a doctor that complains about his patients, a teacher who whines about her students, or a union worker who shakes his fist at *the man.* Those "colleges" might all be pretty discouraging. But the nuns she has encountered are filled with the joy of a newlywed. As a mom, I want that kind of joy for her, no matter what her profession.

More than anything else, I want her to be Catholic.

It's easy to be Catholic some of the time. Everyone's Catholic on Fat Tuesday. But I want my daughter to encounter Catholicism as it should be, so that she will live her faith as it should be lived. For assistance in this, I can count on the fact that she will never meet a lukewarm nun.

Catherine of Sienna once said, "If you are what you should be, you would set the world ablaze." Lukewarmness has no place in a world set ablaze. In fact, those who attend *that* college face a whole different kind of expulsion (Revelation 3:16).

The Church was born from Christ's gift of the Holy Spirit --
as we recall on Pentecost Sunday. Tongues of fire blazed above the disciples, and they couldn't contain the good news. Such a sight would surely rock the average cradle Catholic.

So if my daughter "is what she should be," perhaps she will rock a cradle or two as a mother or as a Sister. Either way, she'll do it as a daughter of her Divine Father, who has every intention of using her to set the world ablaze.

contemplation

When was the last time you talked with your child about his or her future vocation?

Is your child exposed to solid Catholic role models in different vocations? If not, what changes could you make to ensure that they are?

St. Paul tells us in Chapter 8 of his letter to the Romans about those who are "led by the Spirit of God," clarifying that this Spirit does not manifest itself in a spirit of fear or slavery. If your child has received the sacrament of Baptism, then they have this same Spirit within them. And if he or she has been sealed with the Spirit in Confirmation, then becoming "who they are meant to be" is entirely possible. The same applies to you. How are you using that Spirit in your life? Does it manifest itself in courage and steadfastness in your faith as a model to your children? Are they empowered and encouraged as Catholics by your practice of faith?

In what area of your life could you live more courageously in the Spirit?

Pray for yourself. Consider an aspect of your life where it is most difficult to live your Catholic faith courageously. Ask for the Spirit to set your heart ablaze, giving you the courage to face this difficulty and act upon it courageously. Try praying the following Holy Spirit prayer daily and journal about the changes you notice in this area. When your child is struggling with living out their faith courageously, share this experience with him and teach him the Holy Spirit Prayer.

> *Come, Holy Spirit, fill the hearts of Your faithful and enkindle in them the fire of Your love. Send forth Your Spirit and they shall be created, and You shall renew the face of the earth. O God, Who did instruct the hearts of the faithful by the light of the Holy Spirit, grant me in the same Spirit to be truly wise, and ever to rejoice in His consolation. Through Christ our Lord. Amen.*

Pray for your child. Pray for the Spirit to set your child's heart ablaze as well as your own, and discuss with them, the fruit of that prayer on a date.

Think of Catholics you know who are living out their faith in different vocations and professions, and spend time with them along with your children. One way to do this is by hosting a regular game night with other Catholic couples. Your children can engage with them for a short time before shuffling off to leave the adults to a fierce game of Couples Cranium, or better yet, make it a family affair of charades or improv. When they are older then, it will not simply be their parents' marriage that inspires your children to that vocation, but also the examples of loving Catholic marriages they saw modeled in their living room growing up.

THE BENEFITS *of having children*

My husband is a sucker for a three-foot salesman. Lemonade stands, Girl Scout cookies – he can't say no. It's one of the reasons I love him so much. With the arrival of our third child, I was given one more reason to love my husband and thus take advantage of the many perks of having more children.

I was often asked, when we had three whole offspring, if we were "done." To this question I simply responded, "You'd have to ask God," which, I suppose, is better than the grammatical correction that "Turkeys are *done*, people are *finished*."

I'll admit that during moments of great parenting frustration, I have been known to suggest to the Lord that He might not want to push his luck in giving us another, but I would never presume to tell Him his plans. A wise woman once assured me that if I wanted to hear God laugh, I should tell him *my* plans.

I am not entirely sure what a "healthy" attitude toward family size is, except that it involves openness - openness to God's plan and openness to life - and that those two are not mutually exclusive ideas.

In my experience, the former involves a degree of heartache dependent upon the latter. Each morning I am awoken by one of three little voices, and the absence of two I shall never hear until Heaven.

Because of the child behind each little voice, I am a more virtuous person than I would have been without them. That is, my children give me more opportunities to experience the virtues of patience, self-donation, and courage. And while the result of their practice often appears as a frazzled woman in need of a Calgon moment, inside I am changed into someone more like Christ than I otherwise would have been.

We don't have children because we are "ready" or because "it's time" or because we think they will "make us happy" – these are the reasons we buy a dog. We have children because God allows us to, and as a result, we find ourselves enjoying moments of happiness that we wouldn't otherwise know.

One such moment involved our third child and my husband who had suffered a long day at work. Having gotten the other children bathed and in bed so I could get a few things done, I found him slow dancing with his six-week-old girl in the hallway humming an out of tune version of "Amazing Grace" in an attempt to get her to sleep. It was working for both of them as I watched him fight sleep standing up.

There are things I anticipated in having another child: the additional ten minutes I would be late to anywhere, the reality of having one more person than my husband and I, being only two, could carry at any one time, and the increasing comments from strangers like, "Apparently, you don't know what causes that."

What I didn't count on was God's math. In God's arithmetic, love does not divide among an increased number of beloveds. It multiplies exponentially. And that ability to love, in turn, is shared by others.

As a result, a moment of slow dancing between my husband and another woman in the hallway is one hundred times more romantic to me than the night he bent his knee to ask for my hand over a decade ago. And the patience I lacked a decade ago I now practice in coordinating a world-class, unsuccessful lemonade stand three times in the same week, because his children asked me to.

contemplation

What are the specific gifts that each of your children bring to their community? Have you considered that without that child, that particular combination of gifts would be absent from the world?

How open to God's plan for your family have you been in your life? Are there particular situations or moments in which you find it more difficult to be open to His plan than in others (for example, those that deal with finances or relationships)? What do you tend to do in these moments of struggle? What was the result of one such instance when you did not trust in God's plan and inserted your own instead?

Think of one particular time when openness to God's plan reaped surprising benefits in your life. Did you share those benefits with others in some way? What was the result of your sharing them?

What have your choices regarding family size taught your children about God's "math?" Do your kids see children as a blessing from God, or as an asset or possession? Is what you are doing in your family teaching them to open to as many children as God has planned for them one day, or do you think they will only be open to as many as seems "prudent" in society's opinion?

action

Choose one area or situation of your life where you have struggled to trust God's plan. Commit yourself, through prayer and action, to give over any fear in that area and trust him. Keep a "trust journal" and include your feelings along the journey, recording how that openness blessed or changed you and your family. Share your results, if you would like, with your child while out on a date with him or her.

Consider prayerfully what God is calling you and your family to in regards to having more children. Have you done something to shut God out of *your* plan for your family size? Does He want you to consider having more children at this time? Is he calling you to being open to life in another way, perhaps in adoption or foster care? Discuss with your spouse what God reveals to you both in prayer about this, and act accordingly.

THE POWER *of dating parents*

If there is one thing that can never be underestimated – besides the damage one unsupervised little boy can do with a deserted power drill- it's the importance of a married couple that still dates each other.

In marriage, dating cannot be counted a luxury. It is an absolute necessity and can work on any budget and in any situation. No excuses.

My husband and I have two different sorts of date nights. The first requires little effort after the kids go to bed early each Friday. We get takeout from a local restaurant, talk briefly about our week, and then watch the latest DVD to arrive in our mailbox. It's my favorite night of the week.

The other date night is less frequent and much more complicated. It involves recruiting, transporting and paying a reliable teenager to care for our precious cargo. Then there is the strategizing of bottles and dinners for the children, setting out pajamas and toothbrushes, and leaving detailed instructions in case the sitter should need to reach us, our six closest friends, or Poison Control. Really, by the time we leave the house, my husband and I are ready for bed. But we plug on, inspired by the warm feelings we had last time we went to all this trouble.

There are a few things that make this monthly adventure better than even our Friday nights.

The first is planning. My husband is an expert at searching out the best little ethnic restaurant, making reservations if necessary, and keeping it all a surprise until we get there. Of course there are spots we frequent, having found their ambience conducive to two tired parents who are pretending to be put-together adults for a few hours. Whichever is the case, I don't have to do a thing.

The second is budget. Because we have made these dates regular and mandatory in our marriage, we prioritize a portion of our budget for them. This makes any nervous inspection of the menu all but nonexistent. And it brings us back to that blessed free spiritedness in our early years of dating when it was clear that the other person was worth splurging on.

The third is conversation. For our anniversary one year my husband requested a book entitled *Forty Unforgettable Dates with Your Mate.* At the end of each date's description is a list of creative questions to ask one another, like "If money were not an option what dream would you fulfill in your life right now?" They are questions we wouldn't normally ask one another after ten-plus years of marriage, or after the aforementioned fatiguing preparation for a night away from the children.

We also agree that only a portion of the conversation can be about the kids. If there is a big decision to be made about one of them, or even a little silly story worth retelling, we only do so for part the date. The rest of the conversation is given to each other, and to taking the proverbial temperature of our relationship.

Somewhere in the middle of the serious and the impractical, we end up laughing our heads off and I recall the reason I am so lucky to be married to my best friend.

In preserving this dating routine, we do more than nurture our relationship. We set an example.

The faces we kiss before leaving the house know that we are all dressed up and going out to be with each other -- alone. Our hope is that they will see how we honor each other this way, reserving time just for our marriage. Then they will realize that we are more than Mom and Dad; we are Husband and Wife who believe that our most important relationship on earth takes work, and that work can be delightful.

When was the last time you went on a planned, scheduled date with your spouse? Did the preparation for the date show your spouse that they are as worthy of such planning as they were before you were married? How did you feel when the date was finished?

.... *action* ....

Budgeting

If you have not done it already, set aside a portion of your budget for a monthly date night. If the budget is tight, consider a less expensive date at a local coffee shop where you can sit and enjoy each other without having to spend a lot of money. Collect two-for-one dinner coupons from coupon mailings and choose your dinner destination from those restaurants. Budgeting the monthly date may mean cutting out a few other things like less fast food or cutting back on your cable channels. Consider the benefits of such a change and make them. Your spouse is worth it.

Planning

Choose one spouse who will plan the whole date, start to finish, each month and stick to the schedule. The two of you can switch each month if you would like to. (We know a couple who make this a fun competition in their marriage. Each spouse plans six dates a year and at the end of the year, their final date is a sort of "awards show" in which they choose the winner of different categories such as "Most Fun Date for no Money," "Most Creative Date," "Most Unexpected Date," "Most Relaxing Date," etc.)

Atmosphere

Try to make the greater part of each date a situation in which the two of you can dialogue and enjoy each other, rather than just stare at a movie screen before driving home. Keep a notebook of questions that you would like to ask one other and bring it along on your date. Do not to make all of the questions practical. Mix in a few, "Where would you live if you won the Lottery tomorrow?" types.

Babysitters

If a babysitter is necessary, ask that person to write the recurring date into his or her calendar each month (the first Saturday of each month, for example) so that you do not have to find a new sitter each month. Asking a friend or family member can save money here too. We have even had friends swap babysitting each other's children once a month so that both can have a regular monthly date.

Take an annual get-away

Make a plan to get away for an overnight or a weekend together once a year. This can be intimidating if there are small children in the house, I know. There have been years when we have missed this outing because of a new baby and by the year's end, we are keenly aware of having missed it. (That said, we know couples that have been married ten years and not had a weekend alone since their honeymoon because they can always find an excuse not to go!) This annual trip takes more planning than a monthly date, but the result of that retreat together – especially when it is planned and budgeted – is of incalculable benefit to your marriage and family.

KEEPING *wholly the sabbath*

Every year on the Feast of the Holy Family, my family carries on a thirty-year tradition with another family we have grown up with. That tradition is football. Not the kind of football that calls for a remote, a couch, and a large bowl of queso, but the kind that calls for an otherwise queso-eating crowd to dust off their tennis shoes and break out the pig skin.

A few dominant athletes in each family continue to receive the praise and awe from the rest of us, and at the day's end we lick our wounds and discuss the better game plan over barbecue. The game is never pretty, but the tradition is beautiful.

For three decades with few exceptions, this annual gathering has worked to cement relationships built on the faith of parents who found an uncommon feast day worth celebrating. In fact, I often refer to members of the other family as my cousins and their parents as my Aunt and Uncle, rather than the godparents they are. The cousin description has baffled some who see our clearly dissimilar Irish and Lebanese traits, but the real explanation seems too implausible: that our families grew up in two different cultures, on two different sides of town, but always bonded because of our parents' faith. That's when I bring up the Holy Family football game.

When I became a parent, it occurred to me that each Sunday should be a holy family celebration. That is, Sundays are a celebration of our larger family in the Church and a chance for our little domestic church at home to celebrate God's gift of our family members. A continuing theme set forth by our bishop a few years ago on rediscovering Sunday as the Lord's Day, a day set apart for rest and praise, encouraged my husband and me to adopt a few practices for our own family in an effort to become holy.

Ergo, Sunday now also carries the title in our house of Family Fun Day, and will remain so named until my kids can grasp a more appropriate title like Holy Family Day. On Sunday we celebrate family: ourselves as children of a loving Father, siblings of a Saving Brother, and charges of a holy Mother in Mary and the Church. We often continue the celebration after Holy Mass by sharing bagels with another family, and then conclude it with a large family potluck that includes local relatives and other friends bearing a side dish.

I find that with such a schedule, it is nearly impossible to run errands, or write articles, or do other things apart from my family on Sunday. As a result, I am forced to accomplish these tasks on the days that were designed for them: Monday through Saturday.

It's a hard schedule to commit to in a society that purports convenience and flexibility by building four pharmacies within a square mile. It's hard to give one day solely to God and family when I only have six other days to accomplish all that my life requires.

But as I adjust, I find that God makes His way into every day much more easily and my priorities line up much better. Sunday becomes a gift, a sacred respite that recharges me and renews my commitment to my faith and my family.

The richness of Sunday then carries into the rest of the week and truly becomes the end and the beginning, as the Eucharist is the source and summit of our life and faith. We make it His day again, and thank Him for the gifts of rest, of family, and of rare occasions when we win the annual football game.

············· *contemplation* ·············

Have you set the Lord's day apart for rest and worship, or is this the day of the week when your family gets all the things done that they didn't get done Monday through Saturday?

What does the way you spend your Sunday reveal to your children about your gratefulness for all of God's provisions during the week? Do they see any great distinction on this day from the rest of the week? Do they look forward to Sundays as a time of rest, family, community and worship of God?

Do you feel rested and renewed on Monday morning and ready to give your family, your job, and the Lord your best?

Lent is a great time to make the following change to your family's rhythm, because it will involve sacrifice and "offering up" some conveniences, but this can be done any time of the year, and the sooner the better.

Plan your week.
Make a family calendar for the week that is visible to all in the house. Because Sunday is often treated as the last day of the week rather than the first day as it is portrayed in a typical calendar, make your own day-planner-type calendar in which Monday thru Saturday precedes Sunday. Write in all appointments and activities on Monday through Saturday, and color in Sunday as entirely "full." Leaving it blank will tempt you to fill it with some to-do. Once you get this rhythm down, moving Sunday back to its proper place as the first day of the week will help your family focus on the Lord's Day as one of spiritual preparation for the week ahead.

Plan your Sunday.
Have your family plan Sunday's schedule together, beginning with Mass. The idea is not to "over plan" the day and fill it with activities so that the resting is defeated, but to plan restful activities so that the other busy-ness does not creep in. A family who has scheduled brunch after Mass cannot run to the Mall or Home Depot. A family that is gathering for board games or a family movie and popcorn cannot be mowing the lawn or playing catch-up with household chores.

Though Mass is the perfect form of prayer, it need not be the only one on a Sunday. Implementing another simple, regular prayer time in your Sunday family rhythm is crucial to keeping the day's meaning in focus. Try a Divine Mercy Chaplet at 3:00, or a special intentions prayer meeting in midday followed by a rosary.

AVOIDING *the resounding gong*

Most holidays I find fairly simple to share as lessons with my children. Thanksgiving instigates a grateful heart, overflowing like a cornucopia with blessings. Christmas offers the chance to bring the Christ-child back into focus and praise God for the gift of the Incarnation. Easter, of course, recalls for us all that suffering is not in vain, and that there is great hope for those who believe in Christ. Even Labor Day offers a chance to thank the Lord for the chance to serve him with our hands here on Earth.

But I will admit that Valentine's Day throws me for a loop each year. So indoctrinated with Hallmark-isms, heart-shaped chocolates, and the images of two silhouettes dancing to the joy found in a new diamond necklace, I have been at a loss for ways to make the holiday spiritually fulfilling for my kids. Even a brilliant lesson filled with St. Valentine lore about his quest to keep marriage alive in the church seems to pale against the backdrop of red roses and shiny gold boxes of Whitman's Samplers.

But with the release of Pope Benedict XVI's encyclical *Deus Caritas Est*, or "God is Love", I had resolved my Valentine's conundrum. Or at least I thought I had.

I imagine a few other moms know what it is like to get carried away with a "teachable moment." The year this encyclical was released, in an effort to remind others that love is patient and kind, never rude or boastful, I made the kids fluorescent colored T-shirts with big black iron-on letters reading "Deus Caritas Est." I might as well have sent them out with bullhorns. We then decorated heart-shaped cookies with "1 John 4:7" written in frosting to hand out to people. A little over the top perhaps, but I was on a mission against commercialism. And it didn't stop there.

Utilizing innumerable scrapbook tools, I proudly began crafting one-of-a-kind scriptural valentine cards with great care. The effort was largely successful until sticky fingers began to impede the process and disturb my neat assembly line. My patience grew thin and I found myself resenting the fact that no one appreciated my efforts to make these perfect portrayals of the pope's insight into God's idea of love.

At this point, my children had lost interest in the entire Valentine's Day process, and began playing something else. There I was, up to my eyeballs in cardstock, glitter and grommets, wondering again what my intention had been in the first place. It was time for a *Mommy Do-over*.

So the next year I let the two oldest kids choose their valentine design: Cats for my daughter and horses for my son. Resisting the temptation to utilize my rather costly English degree by suggesting clever puns like, "Valentine, you're the cat's meow" or "No Horsin' Around, I love you," we tucked them into envelopes and the project was finished. We then sat down to read from 1 John 4, verse 4, the launch pad for Pope Benedict's encyclical:

> *"God is love, and he who abides in love abides in God, and God abides in him."*

I asked my children what they thought it meant to "love" others. Their small wisdom astonished me. They blurted out things like, "being kind to people," "giving your baby away," and "dying for others." It was inspiring.

At Mass the next Sunday, we listened to St. Paul's two thousand year old description of love which the greatest poets have failed to articulate better: It is patient and kind. It bears all things and endures all things. It's *caritas*, and it does not seek its own interests.

Anything less, even the most gorgeous valentine card, if done without caritas, is a big, fat, resounding gong.

So on the back of each cat and horse was tucked a little piece from scripture which we prayed aloud for the card's recipient: "Let us love one another, since love is of God" (1 John 4:7). And as we did this, their list of recipients grew longer and longer, until we ran completely out of cardstock and glue.

In the end, only a few things remained, and the greatest of these was love.

contemplation

When you celebrate a holiday with family, does your celebration have a Christian focus?

Do you tend to get carried away with holiday preparation to the point of losing focus on why you are celebrating?

Do you or does your family dread the holiday time because it is often exhausting and draining on the budget?

action

Mark out the next holiday coming up, whatever it is. Determine to make a day that focuses on God in your house. There are numerous books in Catholic bookstores and online with ideas on how to make Advent or Lent a more spiritual and less commercial time in your home. Implementing even one or two of them can dramatically change your Christmas and Easter. But there is no need to wait for those two holidays, if another is coming up. Feel free to focus on lesser celebrated ones and determine one way to make it a Christian one in your home.

Websites like www.illuminatedink.com and www.catholicmom.com are very helpful for finding family-friendly ideas for making holidays holy.

FINDING *the better part*

One of the things I love about summer is that it affords me time to be the kind of parent I should probably be all year round: one who stops what I am doing to play with my children, who says yes to messy projects that take longer to clean up than they do to complete, and who has time to sit and ask God, "Is this the better part?"

As an in-remission type-A personality, I ask this question a lot. It comes from meditating on the lives of Mary and Martha, sisters to Lazarus in the New Testament.

In their familiar introduction in the gospel of Luke, Martha is toiling in the kitchen while Mary sits at the feet of Jesus, listening to his words. Martha complains to Jesus and asks him to do something about Mary's idleness when she is gently reminded by him that "only one thing is necessary" and that Mary has chosen "the better part." Many a woman sees this passage of scripture as a sort of litmus test for holiness, considering which of the two women she is most like at different moments of her life.

I won't go as far as other critics who regard Martha's actions as petty, ungrateful, and skewed in their priorities. The Bible tells us that Christ loved her, and she obviously showed her love through her feminine spirit of hospitality. After all, she is *Saint* Martha, and one of only a handful of Christ's disciples to profess aloud that he is the Messiah (cf John 11:27). Further, her intimate friendship with Jesus reveals some of the most honest prayer in the New Testament. After the death of her brother she cries out to Jesus in frustration, "Lord, if you had been here, my brother would not have died. And even now I know that whatever you ask from God, God will give you." (John 11:21-22).

Still, with all those saintly qualities Martha also demonstrates a tendency in many of us to let the details distract from "the better part."

Our daughter once served as a flower girl in a family member's wedding. She looked lovely, all dressed in white with little pearls tucked into her curls. Up to the morning of the wedding I had been pretty clear in explaining to her what her uncle's special day was all about. The beautiful decorations and music, flowers, friends and family who had come from all over, I said, were meant to give witness to the sacrament, and to pray for the start of this couple's vocation to marriage.

But when her curls began to wilt, and the crinoline made her fidgety, the not-so-holy Martha in me took over and almost undid all the earlier amplification of the sacrament's importance. It took a Christ-like friend to set me straight as to "the better part."

As Christians one of the greatest services we can offer one another is a gentle reminder of what is most important, along with assistance with the details when they are necessary. And as parents, we can ask God to reveal "the better part" to us daily, especially when that "extra time" in summer begins to fill up with home improvement projects, over-scheduling of activities, and other things that take away from the gift of time with our children.

Then when He reveals to us that the "better part" is reading a story with them on the couch for the fifth time while those peak task hours in garage slip away, we can feel assured that we are doing the thing that is "necessary:" following a simple invitation to love our children into sainthood in spite of our own imperfections.

.... *contemplation* ....

Are you someone who spends a great deal of time on the details of things, or on the big picture? What sorts of things tend to get you off track from "the better part?"

Think of one recent situation with your family in which you lost sight of the "better part." What exactly happened? Were you the only person affected by your limited vision?

When was the last time that you helped a friend sort out the details and appreciate the big picture of something? What was the result of that?

Take a moment to think of the next time you will be in a situation like the one you thought of above where you lost sight of "the better part." (Not all of these situations are predictable, of course, but if you are someone who tends to get bogged down in details at large family get-to-gethers, for example, think of the next one you have coming up.) What will be the temptation for you to be distracted from truly being present to those whom God has given you to love? Will you worry about the way the house looks if you are hosting an event? Did something happen at a past gathering which you fear will happen or be brought up again? Will you worry about the budget if you have to pay for something at the event? Will an unfinished project nag at you while you are trying to enjoy those around you?

Now offer up those distractions to Christ before they happen. Whatever details need to be worked out ahead of time, ask for help on those from someone you trust. Confide in that same person your tendency to get distracted from the better part and ask them to remind you of this in love when it is necessary. If you are hosting a gathering and in the past have gotten worn out on the details, be honest with those gathered that you are "trying something new" and implement changes to make the whole thing less stressful for yourself. For example, if hosting large full course dinners are your regular get together, make it a potluck or a dessert-only evening. Put someone else in charge of the evening's activities. Use paper plates and plastic ware rather than your good dishes. Invite fewer people if possible. Ask God for the strength to do what love requires each moment that you are shown "the better part" of the situation. Journal about the results of one event in which you took this approach.

AS FOR ME *and my house*

As I packed up the last boxes in what would from then on be called "our old house," I was at once reminded of all the things which had transpired within those walls. My children took their first steps on those floors, the same floors that I watched my husband-turned-daddy pace with a cradled newborn at the wee hours of the night. I couldn't help but wonder how long it would take the new owners to paint over the Jesus the Good Shepherd motif in our daughter's room, overwhelmed by the outnumbering sheep. Gazing around romantically, I was also reminded of all the clichés that seemed to ring true at the time: *Home is where the heart is, or A home is more than a building, it is the love that fills it, or Home is wherever you hang your hat.*

I found it impossible not to be sentimental. And yet, I know at that home is actually much more than some nebulous, Hallmark concept. It is a tangible set of different colored walls and rooms, marred carpet and ceilings, kitchen smells and room temperatures. And most importantly, ours was a place that we asked the Lord to enter, for real, and occupy the rooms with His Spirit. We asked His angels to come and dwell there and have charge over our children.

And this was the place where friends gathered, meals were served, games were played, and prayers were said. Married couples brought their relationships across our threshold, new parents brought their fears and hopes into my living room, and friends and family fumbled with ideas about faith and love and all things practical around our kitchen table.

It was in the midst of these walls that my husband and I declared, *As for us and our house, we will serve the Lord.* And while I understand "house" in the context of Joshua 24:15 is likely referring to the members within it, I also know that my actual house is supposed to serve the God who blessed us with it.

My prayer in that long ago "seller's market" was that we could some-how weed through the offers to find buyers that would use that home to serve the Lord as well.

Surely they would be visited by the persistent pair of Jehovah's Wit-nesses that had frequented our threshold with claims to the Kingdom. In spite of the high temperatures and the well-meaning advice of neighbors, we never turned away dialogue about our Lord and Savior to these two. I was certain they would be back to peruse the hearts of the home's new owners. We prayed often in that house for those two lost souls in hopes that one day they would bring their evangelizing hearts to the Christian Church where Jesus is Lord and God.

The sentiment and romance of all that had been in our "old house," however, was soon overshadowed by the purchase and details of all that would be in our new one. We began to get caught up in the frustrating minutia that follows such a large and important purchase. As priorities were skewed and deadlines continued to mount, each seeming so very important, I became overwhelmed, until a close friend reminded me of Psalm 127:1, *"Unless the LORD builds the house, those who build it labor in vain."*

Our Heavenly Father could not sign the closing papers, get after those last minute repairs, or select the right Home Warranty, but He could focus our hearts on what really mattered: our true home in Heaven. And in doing so He could bring peace to the "temples" of our bodies, and remind us of our greatest ambition in real estate: to dwell in the House of the Lord all the days of our lives.

contemplation

How has your home served the Lord since you have lived there?

Do you look forward to welcome an unexpected guest or does the thought of an unannounced friend dropping by fill you with dread?

How often do you invite friends to gather in your home? When they are there, do they know it is a Christian home by both your behavior and the physical atmosphere of your home?

If your home has not been blessed by a priest or deacon, make this a priority and get it done. This does not need to be a huge event with friends and family if that is stressful to you. Many deacons are available to do a blessing by appointment.

If you have not done so already, choose a spot in the entry or front room of your home and place in it a visual representation of your faith. This reminder is not simply for visitors, but for you as well. Dusting a picture of the Sacred Heart each week, or polishing a cross, is a regular reminder of Who your house is meant to serve. Never underestimate the power of a visual reminder.

Go to your local Catholic bookstore and buy a few pamphlets on your faith to hand to those of other faiths who come by to "share" their faith with you. As they have the same educative purpose, those visitors should not resent your literature, especially when it is offered in kindness. Most importantly, read the literature before you hand it to anyone. "Catholic Pocket Evangelist" by Fr. Mario P. Romero, "Pillar of Fire, Pillar of Truth" published through Catholic Answers, and "What Catholics Believe: A Pocket Catechism" published through Our Sunday Visitor are all wonderful resources to have available for confronting the arguments of door-to-door evangelists, and each booklet contains easy to find scriptural references which Catholics should be able to find. St. Peter admonishes us to "Always be prepared to make a defense to any one who calls you to account for the hope that is in you"... "yet do it with gentleness and reverence." (1 Peter 3:15)

A RECIPE *for relationship*

Each Lent my daughter and I make Stuffed Grape Leaves together. I wish I could say we do this more often together but due to the fact that the Middle Eastern recipe is so time consuming, I am lucky to make it an annual activity. Still, the once-a-year tradition helps us focus on what is important in life, which in the end has only very little to do with the ingredients that brought us there.

It's the process of making the recipe, not a vast number of complicated ingredients, which protracts the whole experience. There isn't a quick way to do it. No step can be omitted and each one must be completed systematically in order for the recipe to turn out well. The whole thing, which can take hours, is a very meditative experience.

I can only credit myself with knowing the proper science of rolling stuffed grape leaves as a result of a dear friend's tutorial. In her Lebanese-American home growing up, recipes like this were part of her daily fare.

During our first lesson, which took hours, we shared stories, laughed, prayed, and even cried together. We engaged in conversation that would not have been possible by texting or emailing, or by updating each other on our Facebook pages. Only by truly being present to one other did we bind our relationship fast.

Because she had grown up doing this, it is no surprise to me that my friend and her seven siblings have remained extremely close – most of them geographically – to their parents, with whom they rolled many a grape leaf.

One of the most damaging mantras of modern Protestantism asserts that salvation is based on *relationship*, not *religion*, as if a person must choose one over the other. In fact, it has become popular in many Bible Churches to teach that a person must despise the latter in order to gain the former. I offer proof in the grape leaves, and in Lent, that quite the opposite is true.

The word religion is rooted in the Latin *religare*, which means "to tie fast or bind together." Like the relationship-binding task of properly rolling grape leaves, our Catholic religion, practiced properly, binds us in relationship to the God who asked us to remain in him (cf. Jn 15:4).

This binding is especially powerful during Lent. For forty days we focus, sometimes for hours, on what it cost God to save us. We make ourselves truly present to Him through fasting, personal sacrifice and prayer. The annual reception of ashes, the predictable changes in the liturgy and readings during Lent, all draw us closer to God in a way that only the time, reflection and presence afforded by these forty days can. In short, if it weren't for our Catholic *religion*, we wouldn't be forced to break the rhythm of our otherwise busy lives in order to meditate again on God's abundant love for us through the sacrifice of His Son.

When we engage in this meditative, religious experience of Lent it is no surprise that by Easter we are closer to God than we were on Ash Wednesday. The entire process helps us focus on what is most important in life, which in the end has only little to do with the ingredients that brought us there.

Rolling grape leaves with my children of course results in a colossal amount of my favorite Middle Eastern appetizer. But it also provides us the experience and reminder of how necessary the practice of specific habits is to maintaining our relationship. If we steadily work on this relationship over a lifetime together, I suspect my children will remain close to me and thus to my Lord and Savior and theirs – like the branches on the vine that they are.

What traditions in your family bind you all together? Do those traditions implement an understanding of your home as being a Christian one?

How does your family embrace the church's traditions during Lent and Advent? Do you participate in things like Ash Wednesday service, Lenten Stations of the Cross, or Advent service projects in your church? Do you typically feel closer to God at Easter and Christmas than you were at the start of Lent and Advent each year?

action

Develop a regular habit of prayer with your family, whether it is a weekly rosary or daily Divine Mercy chaplet before bed. Stick to this for a specified period of time (at least one month), as you will be tempted by scheduling problems and other excuses to drop it after a time. (I shouldn't have to mention that the devil hates a praying family and will do virtually anything to make them stop or get distracted from it.) Make it a prayer time in which everyone participates, whether that means each child saying a decade of the rosary or each person leading the prayer on a certain day of the week. At the end of that time period discuss with your family the benefits they experienced, and consider implementing changes to make this prayer time a permanent one.

Note that not every child will feel it is beneficial to say regular prayer together, so aiming for a democratic decision regarding family prayer may be impossible. As a teenager especially, I found our Friday night weekly rosary inconvenient and cramping to my social life. Today, I see the great fruit of that prayer which was begun and maintained by my parent's dedication to their children's upbringing as Catholics. A child's discontent with regular prayer is not a reason to stop. It may be helpful to journal with them about a trial they are going through and how the regular prayer – when it is used to combat that trial in offering – affects the outcome.

part 2

ON SACRIFICE & OBEDIENCE

THE BLESSING *of little crosses*

Each night my daughter draws a little cross on my forehead, and I do the same on hers just before I turn out her light. First comes mine as I say, "God's angels have charge over you while you sleep." And then I endure her long draw-out rendition of a very detailed cross made with her pinky finger just above my brows.

If it's late enough, I have been known to grow impatient with her artistry. *How long does a cross take?* A few times I have come close to pulling away, impatient and in charge, sure to teach my daughter a lesson that she can't procrastinate falling asleep by dragging out our blessing process. In those times, I fear, I forget that her cross is really a blessing.

My daughter comes from a long line of forehead cross artists. As early as I can recall, my dad was carving crosses on my forehead before I left the house. His rendition was always accompanied by the phrase, "Use good judgment". The ceremony was embarrassing at best when it preceded dates in high school, always in front of the gentleman taking me out. Believe me when I say that, even metaphorically, that cross and phrase were etched into that young man's forehead too before he walked me to the car.

On the way to the car, I would sometimes apologize for my deacon-dad, and laugh uncomfortably, as I thought to myself, *Why does he have to give me those little crosses?* Perhaps that was part of being a deacon's daughter, a casualty all my friends were aware of. Or perhaps I just forgot those little crosses were blessings.

I once heard a priest ask the congregation to reflect upon Mary's answer to God at the Annunciation. The priest asked us to consider that Mary's *fiat*, her yes, would never have been possible without all the little fiats in her life leading up to it.

It occurred to me that the same might be true about little crosses. While we will never be asked to carry the cross of Calvary on our backs, we can be sure that God tests our mettle with the little crosses in order to prepare us for the larger ones.

In the summer of 2005 our family experienced a tremendously heavy cross with the stillbirth our third child, our son Ben. I am quite certain we could never have endured his death were it not for the crosses that prepared us along the way. With each child's sickness, with each small death or loss in our life, we have learned to turn our gaze toward our sovereign Father in Heaven, humbly submitting to His will and wisdom.

The alternative to this submission, I have learned, brings little peace. In our humanity, we want to react to uncontrollable moments of pain or loss by asking, *Why does He have to give me these crosses?* Perhaps within the long process of grieving or addiction we are tempted to ask, *How long does a cross take?* How merciful is our God who reminds us that the greatest virtues are those of humility, patience and trust in Him.

I have committed to introducing little forehead crosses to my children, the same little crosses they received on the day of their baptism. The payoff will be when their gaze turns toward their sovereign Father in hard times, and they can see the little crosses as blessings.

contemplation

Looking back at a heavy loss in your life, can you see any way in which God had prepared you for it? Can you see any gain in your spiritual life or otherwise from this loss?

When small sufferings come your way, how do you deal with them? Do you treat them as larger crosses than they are, or as occasions to become strengthened in your faith?

Does your example in dealing with suffering inspire your children to turn to God in moments of their own trials?

The lives of the saints are a tremendous resource for spiritual training. Many of them have stories of personal struggle, suffering and even societal exile that young people can find inspiring. Adopt a habit reading about the saints together as a family. There are several ways of doing this. The Saint of the Day (available from www.AmericanCatholic.org) can be sent to your inbox and printed out to be read at the dinner table. There are dozens of short collected saint biographies that can be read from daily or weekly. Many of these books are even written for children, though of course they can be found for all ages. Studying an in-depth biography of only a few saints each year is also very beneficial. Reading about and discussing the lives of great men and women of the Catholic faith creates a perspective for suffering and holiness unmatched by even our own accounts.

PACKAGE *for a soldier*

As a general rule, I avoid big sale events. I find shopper mania exhausting, and coupon cutters intimidating. But a few times each year I find myself circling the children's clothing department like a bird of prey, just waiting until the racks can no longer hold their once-reduced merchandise and the store must slash even the clearance price to give way to a real steal.

Beckoned at the start of one summer by such a rack, I ended up with several pair of little boys' pajamas slung over my arm, all of them part of a military theme.

Forget that my son prefers animal rescuers to camouflage and artillery. For 80% off, he can pretend to be G.I. Joe for a night or two. One set even came with a free bag of those little green army men I remember playing with as a child. Whether motivated by nostalgia or the thrice reduced price, I grabbed them without intimation of the eventual lesson they would teach us.

My husband and I haven't talked much in detail about war with our children, in spite of the fact that our country is presently involved in one. Maybe we are afraid that the answers are too complicated or that we will introduce to them new fears we have ourselves. We just pray for the safety of soldiers in general terms and that God would bring a lasting peace to the Middle East. Since most of the prayer falls on sleepy ears at the end of the day, we haven't been asked for additional explanation. That is, until I brought home the new pajamas.

The kids had a great time playing with the little plastic soldiers in the kitchen, lining them up as best they could, given the often poorly crafted plastic bases of each little man. But when I heard them calling the figures knights, and then ninjas, I realized it was time for a little history lesson.

We talked about war and about the brave men and women who volunteer to fight for our country so that we can sit around the kitchen and feel safe as we talk about them. We talked about all those who have given their lives for freedom and goodness and for people like us whom they have never met. And as I briefly but brilliantly danced around political land-mines, citing examples from wars in history that shaped our American character, my five year old just stared at her line of soldiers at eye level. She interrupted me somewhere between WWI and II and asked if some of the men who were fighting today had children.

"Yes," I explained, "and they have chosen to defend our family far away instead of getting to be with their own family here right now."

The weight of that statement hit me and I tried to hide the lump in my throat as I finished it.

Just then, her wobbly soldier toppled.

She looked up and said, "I sure am glad Daddy isn't a soldier."

We both cried then, and took a moment to pray for all the daddies who are soldiers. Then we put together a very special package for a soldier, complete with drawings and goodies and one very special item: a little green army man, hand-selected by the children in our home - one with a sturdy base who doesn't topple easily.

Before I sealed the box, my daughter tucked the little figurine in carefully and told me to include him "so the soldier doesn't forget who he is." I included a cross for the same reason.

The price of sale rack camo pajamas: $4. The cost of sending a care package to a soldier overseas: $25. Having a child realize that freedom isn't free: priceless.

·········· *contemplation* ··········

When was the last time you thanked a member of the military for their service?

When was the last time you prayed for the safety of soldiers fighting overseas?

Do you know someone who has a loved one fighting overseas? Is there something you could do to bring them some comfort as they wait for their loved one to come home (a meal or a prayer bouquet perhaps)?

.... *action* ....

Many churches now have a wall or bulletin board with pictures of military personnel who are family members and those belonging to the parish. Next time you go to Mass with your child, arrive early and look at those photos. Pray for their safety and for their safe return home while you are at Mass, and pray also for their family.

Put together a small care package for a person serving in the military. There are websites that give specific instructions on what can and cannot be in the package, and where and how to send them most efficiently. If your child has the opportunity to simply send a thank you letter to those fighting overseas, this is also a great opportunity for them.

Teach your children to say "thank you for your service" whenever they see a veteran or member of the military. Often, retired veterans wear some sort of insignia or clothing on Veteran's Day, or they may have a VT on their license plate distinguishing them. I have rarely been in an airport without seeing a man in uniform. Our family has seen several different reactions from veterans when we have done this. None have ever been less than gracious. We even saw one man tear up when my son ran across a parking lot to thank him. He could hardly get out the response, "You are certainly welcome, young man."

OBEDIENCE: *path to true freedom?*

It wasn't the first time my Catholic-convert husband had thrown me a zinger. He'd been doing that since the start of our courtship in the Bible Belt of Texas when he began to realize that the teachings of the Church were a bit different from the things he'd been taught about them as a child. This time, however, his question was more rhetorical than those begging doctrinal answers or scriptural reference.

We had just been listening to a radio talk show before dinner in which the caller, claiming to be Catholic, ranted excessively about all of his problems with the Catholic Church.

"First they want to tell us what to do in our bedroom, and now they're all homophobic," the man concluded. "It makes me embarrassed to call myself a Catholic."

I tried to lighten my heavy heart by saying something sarcastic like, "I call myself a runner, but that doesn't mean I've ever seen a marathon start line," but I stopped when I heard my husband.

He shook his formerly-Protestant head, looked into his mashed potatoes and asked me the zinger (or perhaps now that I think of it, he was asking the potatoes).

"Why do Catholics have such a problem with obedience?"

A million dollar question. I, too, looked to the potatoes for an answer. When the spuds offered nothing, I decided to search elsewhere.

It wasn't until weeks later in my daughter's classroom that I discerned a clue which shed light on the truth behind our fallen nature.

A month-long project was underway in which the preschoolers would witness the metamorphosis of caterpillars into butterflies. A small container littered with leaves and five tiny larvae served as a stage for this impressively slow, and yet spectacular event.

These five small pre-insects would transform into exquisitely designed creatures able to soar over views they never knew existed in their primal, sluggish state. The trick is in the conversion: before becoming a free, ascending, beautiful creature, the caterpillar must be bound completely for a time, allowing nature's laws to change him.

The binding is to his advantage. For what caterpillar would be content eating dull leaves in the second stage of his life cycle if he knew what was to come: sweet nectar and heights unimaginable? Obeying the laws of nature, he becomes what he is meant to become: beautiful.

Given a free will, perhaps a few rebellious would-be monarchs might stomp one of their six stumpy feet and attest, "I'm content just being a caterpillar! I don't need some law stifling me and determining what I am supposed to be!" Alas, these creatures are made in the image and likeness of insects, with no free will.

A truth remains nonetheless: Freedom comes with following the rules. In the Church, so does sainthood. Unfortunately, over the past five decades, obedience has transformed from being understood as a virtue to now being considered a pathological condition, and the effect on society has been devastating. As a result, many have settled for license rather than freedom and so have missed out entirely on the beautiful person they are meant to become.

Of course, this rebellion against the beautiful is not new. Disobedience is not a 21st century phenomenon. We all recall the shining Serpent who convinced Eve that what she really desired was the false, the evil, and the very attractive. What she sacrificed, and what man has been searching for ever since, is the true, the good and the beautiful.

Enter the Church's gift of Lent.

Lent is a gift for us Christian caterpillars, a chance for us to be bound for a time and stripped of those things that make us content with anything less than the beautiful. By practicing limits and obedience for forty days we are made more ready to rise at Easter, and to one day fly to a place unimaginable with the One who makes us beautiful.

contemplation

In what area of Catholic Church teaching do you struggle the most with being obedient? What has been the result of your struggle? If you have chosen not to adhere to a certain church teaching, has the result of your decision ultimately been happiness or an unsettling discontentment?

How has your reluctance in this area been an example to your children? Do they see Catholic teaching as a smorgasbord, a place where they can pick and choose what to adhere to? If so, what is this approach to the faith teaching your child about the authority of the Church that Christ established, or for that matter, the power of the Holy Spirit to guide that church? Do they conclude that they were baptized into a faith that doesn't really have the whole truth?

action

Determine an area in which you struggle to be obedient to Catholic Church teaching. Become fully informed on the issue by finding solid Catholic explanations about it, so that you understand the church's motivation on this teaching. Books like Matthew Pinto's *Did Adam and Even Have Belly Buttons?* (written for teens) And Karl Keating's *What Catholics Really Believe: 52 Answers to Common Misconceptions about the Catholic Faith* are great starts to educating on commonly misconceived Catholic teachings. *The Good News about Sex and Marriage* by Christopher West is an excellent resource for those who struggle with the Church's teaching on contraception and the call to marital chastity. It has been said that 98% of people who have a problem with church teaching disagree with their misconception of that teaching rather than the actual teaching itself.

Take your struggle to the Lord through Reconciliation and ask God to give you peace in the truth of His will for you. Journal about your journey in this area and share it with your family if you can.

TITHING *100% obedience*

Imagine if God demanded that ten percent of your health, or ten percent of your years on earth, or ten percent of your children, be returned to him. Most parents would protest, "But I need *all* my health, and *all* my time, so that I can take care of *all* my children! I can't spare any of them!"

At some point, every good parent realizes that their children are not their own. To look into the face of a child is to get a glimpse into God's supreme creativity. How He could come up with those details, all the mechanisms of such a small body that works on its own with only help for nourishment, is awesome. It's a humbling realization for a parent to conclude that just as they didn't create this little life, neither are they in ownership of it.

In 2007 I watched three people lose a father, each in a swift and unpredictable manner. In each case, that father was given little or no time to say goodbye to his children. Surely each man concluded that we do not own our time, or ultimately even our health.

So it would seem that the proper response to a God who would only ask for ten percent of our time, health, or children – and would allow us to keep 90 percent of each - should be not merely submission, but gratitude. But as it turns out, God does not ask for a percentage of any of these.

What He does ask for, evident in multiple places in scripture, is a percentage of our treasure. There is some debate about how this exactly translates into our finances; whether a *tithe* actually means ten percent of our gross or net income, and how much of that should go to the church and how much to other charitable or worthwhile organizations.

Truthfully, I don't know who's debating. But methinks those folks, like the agnostic W.C. Fields on his deathbed with a Bible in hand, are "lookin' for loopholes."

One thing I had to submit to early in my marriage my husband's idea of tithing. "Ten percent off the gross, straight to church and charity," the then-Protestant stated plainly. Aghast, I returned with myriad arguments, beginning with my college loans and debt, and ending with several tithing loopholes I had myself discovered through some miserly advisors. But he asked me to trust him, assuring me that God had always taken care of him in the past. From that day we began the practice of writing our tithe check before ever even looking at the bills.

The process was terrifying at first, since I knew my teacher's salary and his fluctuating sales income could only stretch so far. Over time, however, I noticed that we were indeed well taken care of, even more so than when I was giving much less to the church. To me it seemed a miracle.

As a result of placing one hundred percent of our trust in God, and only ten percent of our income, we have come to use the other ninety percent much better. I have also come to understand that tithing isn't so much about paying the church's very real bills as it is about trusting. It begins with stepping out of the comfortable and really putting our faith in God. As the great author Fyodor Dostoevsky put it, "Faith is not born from miracles, but miracles from faith."

The Magi in the New Testament are a consummate example of this kind of faith. They spent days journeying to see the newborn king of the Jews, bringing with them valuable gifts -- in fact, treasure. They were men of science and reason and yet faith led them to leave their comfortable home and journey toward the uncertain. What they witnessed was a miracle.

God waits for us to act on faith, with our hearts and with our treasure, since the latter, we are told, indicates the former (Matthew 6:21). When we trust Him entirely with both, miracles happen.

What is your current practice of tithing and what principle is it based upon? Does it fluctuate depending on your financial situation at the time or is it more consistent than that?

What does your approach to tithing teach your children about your trust in God's provision, and your stewardship of his gifts? Do they think they have earned all that they have, and that it is theirs to do with as they please?

Spend one week pondering the following scriptures. Write them on a note card and put them up at work where you can see them. Tuck them inside your checkbook, or anywhere you go to make a payment for your bills. Commit these to memory.

> *"Behold, to the LORD your God belong heaven and the heaven of heavens, the earth with all that is in it." (Deuteronomy 10:14)*

> *"Thine, O LORD, is the greatness, and the power, and the glory, and the victory, and the majesty; for all that is in the heavens and in the earth is thine; thine is the kingdom, O LORD, and thou art exalted as head above all. Both riches and honor come from thee, and thou rulest over all. In thy hand are power and might; and in thy hand it is to make great and to give strength to all."*
> *(1 Chronicles 29:11-12)*

Once these have been written on your heart, pray earnestly about your approach to tithing. Ask God to help you trust him with your finances, and ask Him to show you how they can best serve His kingdom. Act on what He shows you. From this practice will come a peace that surpasses understanding.

Journal about and share any growth in this area with your family.

FINDING *your secondary ministry*

Let's be clear: God has called all parents to the primary ministry of family, of raising their kids in the way they should go (cf. Proverbs 22:6). Husbands, your ministry is also etched out pretty clearly in Ephesians 5: Love your wives as Christ loves the Church. Wives, our ministry is detailed thoroughly, if intimidatingly, in Proverbs 31. But if all the husbands, wives and parents are content with fulfilling only their primary ministry, who is going to help with all that work in the vineyard? This is, I think, where secondary ministry comes in.

In our secondary ministry work with engaged couples, my husband and I tell the couples that the best thing they can do after arriving home from their honeymoon is walk into their parish office and sign up for a ministry together. This goes for those who are far from the Lord, those who are close to Him, and to those somewhere in between. The reason for this advice is that any honest effort in that ministry will work to dispel the selfishness and "loss-of-self syndrome" that can often sneak into the first year of marriage.

The work of secondary ministry is not easy, of course. If there is one consistency in the ministry work my husband and I do, it is that the week prior to meeting with couples, we will be filled with disappointments in our relationship. In general, each of us becomes acutely aware of the many ways in which the other person falls short of perfection. As a result we are overcome with a grand sense of hypocrisy, questioning why we are even involved in God's plan to prepare others for the vocation of marriage.

Whenever I explain this phenomenon to other couples involved in the same ministry work, I am overwhelmed at the number of nodding heads. Apparently we are not only joined in our imperfect practice of marriage, but also in our keen awareness of it.

Still, like the other couples, we remain in this ministry, and the work God does through our evolving marriage is always generous. As it turns out, all He really needs from us is that we show up without our egos.

But even showing up can be a trial. Scheduling a babysitter on week-nights, or dragging our children in their pajamas to childcare can be discouraging, making us question whether this season of our lives should really be spent serving those outside our family in such a way. But the answer comes back loud and clear each time we do, usually in the words of a nervous bride- or groom-to-be who only initially agreed to go through marriage preparation in the church in order to appease a fiancé or parent.

"Thanks. I didn't want to be here, but I'm glad we came now. I'd never heard this view of marriage before."

Then we are glad we came, too. Glad we didn't let the nagging sense of hypocrisy talk us out of it. Not because we changed anyone, but because God changed us. He made our marriage - in spite of our many imperfec-tions and our busy schedules - salt and light. And if we had given in to the devil's plan to discourage us, that bride or groom-to-be might have missed God's plan for his marriage. Because the same 30 lay people in each parish working tirelessly for God's kingdom shouldn't have to do it alone. By listening to God's call for us to engage in secondary ministry, we help to make it 32.

Each of us must listen intently to the Lord's call to a secondary min-istry during each season of our lives. The ministry may change and should never detract from our primary vocation of motherhood, father-hood, and spouse.

The process of listening is easier if we recall something: committing to a secondary ministry does not end in sacrifice; it begins there. The end is something we shall not know this side of heaven, but we can hope it will result in our hearing the words, "Well done, good and faithful servant" (Matthew 25:23).

In what ministries have you (or you and your spouse together) participated? Was your net experience in those ministries positive or negative?

Have you ever spent yourself on ministry to the detriment of your
family? Was your participation in that ministry the result of prayerful
consideration, or of some other desire to be of service or to be needed?
Have you ever "stayed too long" in a ministry when it was clear that
God was asking you to do something else?

Have you been asked recently to participate in a ministry or felt God
tugging at your heart to do so? Have you prayed about it?

What fears or anxieties do you have about being called to a secondary
ministry?

.... *action* ....

Think of a time when you were excited to be called to a ministry. Journal about that feeling.

God is always calling us to ministry. It is our great commission while
we are on the Earth. Sometimes that ministry is simply within the walls
of our own home, particularly if a family member is going through a
difficult time. When His call extends to ministry outside the home, this
is also for the benefit of those in our family and never to their detriment. If you have not participated in a secondary ministry for over a
year, ask yourself why. If the answer is something other than a great
need in your family, ask God to reveal to you exactly what he wants
from you in this area of your life. For assistance in this, consider the
following occasions in God's Word where others were called to service
apart from their family.

> *Women: Read the calling of Esther (Esther, Chapter 4) and ask God
> if now you are being called for "such a time as this" to participate in
> a secondary ministry.*

Men: Read the calling of Samuel (1 Samuel, Chapter 3). Ask God to reveal to you His calling for you to ministry at this point in your life. Consider dialoguing about this with a trusted friend whose prayer life aids his judgement.

Though it should go without saying, I shall say it nonetheless: make no decision about ministry work without consulting your spouse. The two of you know your family's needs and dialoguing in prayer about this is of great worth to all who will benefit from any secondary ministry work in which you participate.

part 3

ON SACRAMENTS & LITURGICAL LIFE

PRUNING *your spiritual weeds*

Weed season means a few things in the Moore household. First, it means a blessed ignorance dominates our work outside since our children do not realize how much a landscape maintenance company could earn by doing the same work they will do for a toy from the Dollar Store. It also means that Spring has arrived, and even pulling weeds is a welcome activity in the 80 degrees that heralds Arizona's triple digits. And it also means one more teachable moment in our quest to nurture the little souls of our children.

I have told our two oldest workers that weeds are funny things. They start out very little, and they can blend in so as to go unnoticed for most of the day. There is a certain time of the day, however, when the light hits them in such a way that each one is revealed.

In many ways, I tell them, weeds resemble our sin. The danger in letting little sins go on too long is that they can become so big that it becomes difficult to get rid of them with simple maintenance. And just as weed begets weed, so does sin beget sin.

I want our children to understand that a serious sin is not committed out of nowhere, but is usually the result of smaller sins unconfessed. My hope is that we are sowing good seed in this outdoor lesson. My prayer is that they will develop a great desire for the sacrament of Reconciliation out of a thirst for grace.

Unfortunately for many Catholics, I think, the sacrament of Reconciliation has become a somewhat bothersome task of their faith, an obligation that is only really expected of them once a year. So as a result, many have convinced themselves that only serious sins need confessing. But the tragic result of not availing oneself the sacrament regularly is not that they will be considered a "bad Catholic;" it is that they unnecessarily sacrifice of the grace available through it.

I am not certain why some people stop going to Confession. I suppose for a few it is scheduling issues. Perhaps for others, it is a Protestant-adopted approach to sin which says that we can just as easily confess our sins directly to God without "going through" a priest. But I have to wonder if it isn't also simply a result of living in the same shadowy light as many others who are missing the grace. That is, if everyone you know has an excuse for not going to Confession, one that hinges on its minimal yearly requirement, then it's harder to make out the weeds in your own yard.

Unless, of course, you are a parent.

In the book of Tobit, Tobiah is often referred to as the "light" of his parents' eyes, and I can guess why. I live in the direct rays of my own children, and the result is a clear view of the weeds.

I know when I need to go to confession the way some people realize they need an adjustment from their chiropractor. I get out of whack, often becoming more critical and less patient, and sometimes saying things that sound as if they came out of another person's mouth. I have told my children this before, and to my dismay, they have reacted – more than once in public - to my impatience with, "Mom, I think you need to go to Confession."

And so I go, and the Lord removes my sin, root and all. And the grace I receive spills over into my children. And my patience begets their patience, making us all better at the smaller things involved with the work of family life. Even yard maintenance.

.... *contemplation* ....

What is your view of the sacrament of Penance? Does your practice (or lack) of receiving the sacrament reflect this view? In other words, do you view Penance as a lifeline for grace in your busy life and therefore receive it as often as you can, or do you see it as a bothersome obligation that doesn't really have an affect on your overall state of grace and therefore only receive it when it is "traditionally" offered once a year?

What does your practice of this aspect of your Catholic faith tell your children about their need for God's forgiveness and grace in order to maintain a wholesome spirituality? Do they know when you receive the Sacrament, or do you keep it to yourself? Have you ever invited your child to go to Confession with you?

.... *action* ....

If you have not been going to Confession regularly, ask yourself why and be honest about the answer. Guilt, inconvenience, embarrassment and apathy are all common excuses that God already knows about anyway. Now, go. Address this reason while you are in Confession, and offer it up to God. I have heard a dozen priests tell RCIA candidates that there is not a sin they have not heard confessed before, and I would bet the same goes for excuses. Each one will be received in love and forgiven.

Look in your church bulletin or call the office and find out when Confessions are available. Do this for several parishes in your area so that you have a list of available times for Confession. A Catholic with options has less excuses. If still none of the times work for you, call the church office for an appointment with a priest. You can do this at any church if you are hesitant to go to Confession with a priest you see often.

Set a date for regular confession. My husband and I alternate each month on a certain Saturday making sure that each of us gets there at least six times a year. As a convert to the faith, my husband struggled with the idea of Reconciliation for some time, but regular reception of the sacrament, he will tell you, has changed him tremendously.

A thorough Examination of Conscience is paramount to making a good confession, but there is no need to wait until the actual sacrament to begin this exercise. Many of the saints made this a daily spiritual exercise. It is also a way to take the virtual pulse of your relationships at any time and when practiced regularly, helps you see the significance of your words and actions, which is an immeasurable tool for a parent.

Journal about your journey in this Sacrament over the course of a year and share it with your child if they struggle with the sacrament.

If your child has made their First Reconciliation, invite them to go along with you the next time you go to Confession. I use the word "invite" loosely here. There are different parental theories on this, I know. There are good parents who believe that since Reconciliation is a voluntary opportunity for grace, they should not *force* their child to go. I am a little different on this. The only option my children have is to choose to go with their dad one month or their mom the next, but either way, they are going at least six times a year. For the same reason that I asked the church to pour freezing cold water over my screaming infant's head at baptism, I require them as long as they are under my roof, to go to the confessional regularly. I want them to receive grace as often as possible, because it's hard to be a kid. And I especially want them to receive it when they don't want it, which is generally when they need it most. Our daughter chooses to go far more often because the grace she receives from the sacrament brings her a palpable joy. Studies have shown that children who attended Confession regularly while growing up are more likely to continue doing so when they are away from their family at college. And any opportunity to get a college kid to walk through the door of a Catholic church when he doesn't have to is one that interests me immensely.

HOLD ON LOOSELY:
how a parent's vocation can foster a child's

Since our oldest was very small, she has loved to draw pictures. Her younger brother loves to do whatever his sister does. It is really very sweet. So are the drawings. In fact, I am sure they each have a rare and brilliant artistic talent unmatched by other children their age. But perhaps I lack objectivity.

Even sweeter than the drawings is what our children do with the pictures after they are finished.

Immediately upon completion, if not pre-determined during the course of composition, the masterpiece is hung on the refrigerator and designated as a gift for someone. Each precious painting or portrait is established as a present to be parted with, often to the dismay of this mother who would like to preserve a few for memory's sake. I am permitted only the presents made for me. The rest all go.

I concede to this youngster justice because it teaches me an important lesson about God's goodness.

I am aware of His goodness every morning at the sight of my children's little faces. I am also aware of my unworthiness as its recipient. So like the psalmist, I ask, "What shall I render to the LORD for all his bounty to me?" (Psalm 116:12)

The answer, as I am shown by my children's drawings, is simple: give the good away.

The psalmist also writes, "Children are a heritage from the Lord." (Psalm 127:3). We are meant to give our gifts back to the Lord. What better way to do this than to cultivate the gifts our children have been given? In other words, "Train up a child in the way he should go" (Proverbs 22:6) including the way of vocations to the priesthood and religious life.

One way in which we cultivate this possible vocation in our family is by spending time around priests whenever we can, inviting them over for dinner or giving them hugs after Mass. I want my son to see the priesthood as a vocation as attractive as marriage, as fulfilling as any profession that gives our talents and gifts back to the God who gave them to us. I want my daughter to see the Poor Clare Sisters' black and brown habits as just as beautiful as a white wedding dress. As a parent, I must give my children, my gifts, back to the God who gave them to us -- not unlike Samuel's mother Hannah in the Old Testament.

If this all makes me sound very noble, it's because you didn't see me on my daughter's first day of preschool, arms wrapped around her little waist and white-knuckled in my grip at the classroom door. It is hard to give them away to anyone, even briefly. In doing so, I have to hope that another person will care for them and see them for the gifts they are.

The first step in this surrender is recognizing a simple truth: my children are not mine. For however long or short a time I am given with them on earth, I am meant to be a shepherd and not an owner.

As parents we must remember that God does the *creating* and the *calling* and we are to do the *cultivating*. Perhaps the greatest frustrations in parenting occur when we get those roles confused.

God in His goodness allows us many letting-go's in order that we might truly appreciate what we have been given to begin with: a gift.

So I give away pictures that I would rather keep. I slip my fingers off the classroom door jamb and trust. And I use the time I have with my children to cultivate their gifts until that day when they will be able to give a total gift of themselves in the vocation God has called them to... as priest, as husband, as wife, as His.

When was the last time you prayed about your child's vocation? Have you considered that your most important job as a parent is to love and prepare them for this vocation?

When you imagine your child leaving for school, or for their vocation or profession, how do you feel? Do you have a great sense of sadness and loss, or a healthy sense of accomplishment and desire for them to fulfill God's calling for themself?

How have you fostered God's calling for your child? Do you discuss it with them? Have you asked your son if he has considered the priesthood, and encouraged him to pursue that calling if he has? Have you asked your daughter if she has felt a calling toward marriage or religious life? Does she feel comfortable coming to you with questions or doubts about a calling? Do you have a trusted person to whom you can refer them with any questions you can't answer?

.... *action* ....

If your child is old enough, arrange for them to go on a vocational discernment retreat. Many dioceses offer one-day or weekend-long retreats for such a purpose. It is hard for anyone, especially a busy teenager in a loud environment, to hear God's call without the proper setting.

The next opportunity you have, attend a retreat yourself, even if it means simply getting away by yourself for a day. A guided silent retreat offers a unique opportunity for the Holy Spirit to speak clearly to you, and they may be offered occasionally by religious orders in your area. During your time away, ask God to help you clearly discern what He is asking of you as a parent in your child's life at this moment. Ask Him to open the lines of communication if they have been closed, or to enhance them to include such discussions as their vocation to married or religious life. Many teenagers can have a narrow vision of their future, one that can't see past their present friends and situations. Discerning a vocation does more than give them direction, it offers a unique perspective that commands their preparation now. This is different than the time-specific preparation for career training or higher education which they can postpone until that stage of their life.

THREE WORDS THAT WILL BRING YOU CLOSER TO CHRIST: *offer it up*

If you grew up with a good Catholic mom like I did, you heard the following phrase a lot: "Offer it up." It was issued for any number of reasons, like a get out of jail free card for a mom who was tired of hearing the whining related to our thirst, hunger or boredom. And it sure beat the alternative three words that lesser moms might say, "Zip your trap."

I find myself quoting my mom quite a bit now that I am a parent, and one of my favorite phrases is in fact *Offer it up*. Avoiding those other three words not only keeps me from getting ousted from the Mother of the Year club I pretend to belong to, but it holds me accountable as my children will only practice such self-denial if they see it modeled by a the one who asked it of them.

As the quintessential multitasker, I listen to books while I run, pray the rosary while I clean house, and fight insanity while grocery shopping with children. So when I realized why Catholics "offer it up," I was thrilled.

While giving something up can be healthy in itself, bearing the loss with meekness does something else. It helps us to achieve sanctification.

St. Francis de Sales, a 16th Century bishop and Doctor of the Church who spent much of his time "in the world and not of it," gave the kind of advice for individual sanctification that I only wish someone had told me at my first child's baby shower. It might have saved a few years of heartache.

He wrote to a friend who was experiencing domestic suffering, "The many troubles in your household will tend to your edification, if you strive to bear them all in gentleness, patience, and kindness. Keep this ever before you, and remember constantly that God's loving eyes are upon you amid all these little worries and vexations, watching whether you take them as He would desire. *Offer up all such occasions to Him*, and if sometimes you are put out, and give way to impatience, do not be discouraged, but make haste to regain your lost composure."

I am certain the letter could have been entitled, "To Mary Moore, on the Occasion of Potty Training Her Children."

Many of the saints believed that we could actually offer up our sufferings and unite them Christ on the Cross, and in doing so we achieve sanctification for ourselves and others.

Contrast this redemptive suffering with three other words: *Count the cost.*

We live in a world that would have every suffering person pour their heart out on the Oprah Winfrey show, claim victimization with audience encouragement, and then become instantly compensated, or at least pacified, by a smashing makeover and an iPhone. And there is no shortage of medical doctors, even naturopaths, to be solicited for the cure to nearly every ailment which they see as compromising one's quality of life.

With such a panoply of solutions offering a virtually painless life, why would Catholics choose to voluntarily suffer, especially as a habit during Lent?

Simply put, by fasting or committing to some small voluntary sacrifice we "put on Christ" and join with him in suffering. It makes us humble, countercultural, and Christ*like.*

The other great gain of redemptive suffering is that, practiced regularly, it disciplines us to withstand even greater sufferings that result from our living in a fallen world. And for a parent, the strength we gain from taking up our cross in those situations goes beyond our own sanctification. The little eyes that watch us see an image of Christ, who as we recall during the preparation of the gifts at Mass, "humbled himself to share in our humanity."

Then the faith for which our children may one day be ridiculed will be for them a real manifestation of love because they saw it lived out by others who were humble, countercultural, and Christ-like.

contemplation

Think about the last time you experienced a small suffering or inconvenience. Perhaps it was misplacing your car keys recently, having to wait in line behind someone who didn't seem to have it "all together," or having to repeat yourself when asking your child to do something.

What was your reaction to that suffering? Was it a patient endurance or something more like exasperation? Did your example of dealing with that suffering inspire any onlookers to be more patient in their own little hardships, or did your example make them feel their own suffering even more and perhaps even join in complaining with you?

action

Choose to voluntarily suffer from something this week. For a whole week, choose to go without a convenience like your morning coffee, or your Blackberry, or even baby wipes (this would be a real sacrifice in our home!). Choose something for which to offer up your discomfort, like perhaps an ill friend or family member, your child's vocation, or the spiritual uplifting of your parish priest. When moments of temptation arise to complain about something, try reciting this simple prayer: "Jesus, I trust in you" several times until you recollect why you began this sacrifice.

Journal each evening about your feelings that day and ways in which you offered it up. Include any observations of your children or others regarding your behavior. (This is not a brag log, but a way to see how our self-discipline can affect those we encounter on a regular basis.) Record whether or not, by the week's end, your ability to withstand and even embrace suffering increased, and be sure to include any other benefits you witnessed from this week-long challenge.

DECLUTTERING *for the resurrection*

One year for Lent I went without email, search engines, or updates on world affairs via internet. It was an ongoing affliction to give up the computer for a whole forty days, but I offered it up for the sanctification of my children, for an increase in vocations to the priesthood, and for the salvation of Britney Spears so the whole world can be at peace about that poor girl.

Earlier that same year, my husband gave me one of the best gifts he has ever given me: a four-hour session with a professional organizer. Weeks into a room conversion, I had been at a standstill. Surrounded by boxes of keepsakes, crafts, to-do's, books I intended to read before I turned 90, and a mass of tchotchkes, I lost the ability to prioritize. It all seemed so very important. But after just a short time with a professional, I was made aware of my great impediment to organization: counting too many things as important.

What I gained from her help was both a de-cluttered space and the tools to keep it that way. After whittling out much of what was not essential, I was able to gain perspective and ultimately a bit of peace. It was a process I have since applied to other areas of my life, and one of the reasons I so appreciate the Church's gift of Lent.

As sinners, what we are asking God for during these forty days is a change of heart. Like the Psalmist David, we desire a "clean heart" and a "steadfast, willing spirit." (Ps. 51) In other words, we want a de-cluttered space and the tools to keep it that way.

De-clutterring our hearts and minds during Lent has one supreme effect: it makes room for the message of the Resurrection. In a culture that places great emphasis and expense on hyping the winners of reality TV talent shows, presidential primary election results, and the release of the next best, more streamlined personal electronic device, even a message as essential as God's saving love can get lost.

Whether it is through ashes, fasting, or some small personal sacrifice for forty days, Lent pulls us out of the "ordinary time" into a period of purification, so that the message of the Resurrection does not fall on cluttered hearts. And if the great fruit of fasting is clarity, then that Lent I gained clarity on a few things.

Perhaps the greatest insight came from living without internet searching capability, leaving me with a timely dependence on another superlative resource: God's word.

As it often happens, shortly after determining what I would relinquish for Lent, a great need for that thing arose. A weighty decision had to be made regarding one of our children's medical care, and I was unable to equip myself with information from appropriate websites or parent discussion boards.

I was going to have to ask someone, in person, for advice.

I knew no shortage of opinions would exist among friends and family, but I decided to ask the God who made this child and chose us for her parents, for not just clarity, but peace with our final decision.

I picked up my Bible unsure of where to look. Hedging my bets on a sort of "Bible roulette" I opened to the middle, to Psalm 51.

What happened then can only be likened to the experience of removing every piece of furniture in a room except two chairs: one for God, one for me. Rather than seeking a one-shot answer from God as I had in the past, allowing Him to interject between web searches and others' advice, I found myself in a peaceful dialogue with Him as He worked to whittle out the unessential and create in me a "steadfast spirit" necessary to being a parent. The final result was indeed peace.

When we de-clutter our hearts during Lent, we discover not only what we are able to live without, but ultimately what gives us life: God's eternal promise revealed in the Resurrection.

What spaces of your home collect the most clutter? Do you have a space in your home in which you can sit and pray without the distraction of clutter?

In what areas of your life do you find it hardest to focus? Your spiritual life? Your finances? The needs of your individual family members?

action

Choose one small spot in your home, like a desk drawer or medicine cabinet, that is filled with unnecessary clutter. Set a timer for twenty minutes. Empty the area completely and wipe it clean. Separate the contents into three piles: things that actually belong in that spot (this includes things that you need or have used in the past year), things that belong elsewhere in the house, and things you don't or can't use (items that are broken, expired, or that you haven't used in the past year). Put away the things that belong in that space neatly. Put away ALL the other things that belong elsewhere. Toss, recycle or give away the things you don't use. Enjoy your clean space.

Read Psalm 51:7-14 several times and journal about your reactions. Ask God to reveal to you exactly what you could be doing with a "clean heart" and "steadfast spirit." Go to Confession. Then read the verses again. Meditate on these words for the week and journal about what God reveals to you. The next week, read verses 15-19 and ask God to help you use this clean heart and steadfast spirit in your family, in your workplace, and in your social circle. As you begin to act on His revelation, write down your observations. Specifically, address the question, *"What have I done with this clean heart and steadfast spirit that I could not have done before without it?"*

CHOOSING *a godparent*

John Paul II was certainly correct when he stated, "Parents must be acknowledged as the first and foremost educators of their children. Their role as educators is so decisive that scarcely anything can compensate for their failure in it."

Well said. Still, more than my own wisdom, preparation, and struggle for holiness, I have come to count on two things for my children's welfare: grace and guardian angels. And one great source of grace for every Catholic is the prayers of a godparent.

Upon turning another year older one year, I was patted on the back by a man who assured me I had earned every day thus far. Personally, I think that's selling my guardian angels and my godparents short.

Like most folks, if I were left to my own devices, I wouldn't be where I am today. Grace and guardian angels truly tip the scales in our favor.

Given the difference a godparent can make in the life of a Catholic, I think their role is worth a second look. Because if I am not mistaken, there is a great number of parents out there wondering what exactly constitutes a good choice for a godparent.

The Catholic Church teaches that a godparent should be a trustworthy witness of the faith who will help the godchild attain salvation, and that they are entrusted with a special responsibility: participating in the child's Christian life, formation and education.

Practically speaking, a godparent's number one job is prayer. It's not guardianship, or remembering to send cards and money on their godchild's birthday. It's advocacy for grace.

As a mom of several very adventurous little souls, I know how much of a role grace plays in their safety and their upbringing in the faith. Consequently, my husband and I have our children's godparents on speed dial. Each one has been summoned to prayer on our way to the Emergency Room, or after a grace-made-possible hair's escape from, and even once from inside a bedroom closet during a mommy meltdown while potty training. In the first five years, I am certain the godparents of my son – who made the Energizer Bunny look like Pa Kettle – wore out the knees of several pairs of pants in advocacy.

Knowing then the serious dependency we have on these individuals for our children's salvation, the discernment involved in choosing them, for us, begins the moment the pregnancy test turns positive.

First, we look for faithful Catholics with a devoted prayer life. Second, we look for each one to be a righteous, or virtuous, person, because scripture tells us that "the fervent prayer of a righteous person is very powerful," (Jas 5:16) and we are counting on that prayer.

Finally, we make our request to that person clear: "What we are asking of you is prayer. Not days at the ballpark, not presents, but prayer." Those who have accepted, I believe, understand our requirement to be the more demanding.

Traditionally, many people choose a family member or close friend to be a godparent as a title of honor or a way to incorporate them in a special way into the baby's baptism day. The role becomes predominately ceremonial. In many cases, the godparent is not fully aware of, or perhaps forgets after time, their role in the child's salvation.

In such a case there is still great opportunity for everyone involved to grow in faith, and that is *Re-birthdays*.

Re-birthdays have become a fairly big deal in our house. A re-birthday is the day we recall a child's baptism, the day they were "born again" by water and the spirit. We bake a cake and place the baptism candle in the center before blowing it out. We also take out their baptismal gown and look at pictures of their first sacrament. We discuss how on that day we "claimed them for Christ."

Here are a few suggestions for making the most of this opportunity. First, invite the godparents to celebrate if they live nearby. Explain to your child why their godparents are so important to them, and have the child make a card for them. If they are not doing it already, encourage your child to intercede during bedtime prayer for their godparents.

As a gift on the re-birthday, consider giving the godparents a book on prayer or on your child's patron saint if they are named after one, a rosary, a booklet on how to pray a certain devotion like the Divine Mercy Chaplet, or simply a daily devotional. Encouraging someone's prayer life should be one of the greatest gifts we can give, and should never come across as condescending. One of the finest compliments I received from a person I admire was his suggestion that we continue to "pray for one another." He encouraged my prayer life in doing so, and we became accountable in a way to one another for our walk in holiness. What an honor and responsibility.

A prayerful godparent will grow in spirituality, making them an even stronger advocate. And perhaps such a godparent can even save a guardian angel a bit of trouble.

contemplation

When was the last time you communicated with your child's godparent about your child's spiritual life? Do you share your child's struggles (when appropriate) or prayer requests with them? Do you hold that godparent accountable for the promises they made on your child's baptism, to pray for the child, and to encourage the child to grow in faith and as a member of the church?

Do you need to mend a relationship with a child's godparent?

Have you prayed for your child's godparent lately? Have you asked your child to?

action

Write the dates of all your children's baptisms in your calendar and begin to celebrate Re-birthdays. Use some or all of the suggestions above.

For your child's godparent. Begin to pray with your child for their godparent. If it has been a while since you talked with them about your child's spiritual life, invite them to share a cup of coffee and bring up the issue. Mention that you are working on praying with your child for them also, and ask if there are any specific things you can lift up in prayer.

If your child has a particularly prayerful and involved godparent who asks for ways in which they can be of spiritual service, consider asking them to keep a simple prayer journal for the child that can be presented to them at a pivotal time in their life, like a graduation or wedding or their own child's baptism. What a great gift it would be for that child at eighteen to see that his vocation or safety or friendships were being lifted up when he was nine years old and he didn't even know it. This is a powerful way for that child to see how God has worked retrospectively in his life through another person's prayers.

If you are a godparent. Consider keeping a prayer journal for your godchild like the one mentioned in the paragraph above. Keep a regular time to record in it, like on Sunday evenings before bedtime. Perhaps the readings at Mass conjured a thought for them that you want to write down, or a particular grace you are asking God to bestow on them. Include in the journal anything positive you notice about their spiritual life as well, even if it is just a passing thought mentioned to you by their parents. Pray for that specifically and record your prayer.

MARRIAGE PREPARATION
begins sooner than you think

With the ongoing menaces of economic instability and major social issues hanging in the balance, this might be a good time to turn our eyes toward a domestic issue over which we have more immediate control: the next generation of women living in our homes. In fact, while home has always been the best, it may soon be the only place where the cultural devaluing of true femininity can be cured.

When I was very young I wanted to marry Gene Kelly, but only because apparently Captain von Trapp was unavailable. To me these were the perfect men: handsome, strong, and unabashed in showing their love for a woman, even if it meant singing in the rain. As is the case with many young women, at some point my ideal man began to look a lot like the real one living in my home, my dad.

It takes little research to discover that most women marry a man who is like her father in one way or another. In fact, one of the great responsibilities of fathers is to model qualities of his daughter's future husband.

My husband has no penchant for musicals, rainy or not, but he embraces his role as father and husband wholeheartedly. To my mind, this places him leagues above the late Mr. Kelly.

Each night my husband tucks our seven-year old daughter into bed and speaks to her the last words she will hear that day. He catalogs all the gifts and the talents he saw her use that day, and then concludes by telling her how beautiful she is. Sometime later in our busy schedule, I will do my best champion her daddy's nightly message. I assure her, that besides being a treasured daughter, she will one day make a lovely bride.

Simply put, every girl is meant to be a bride. She is created above all other purposes to be in union and communion with her spouse. Ultimately, she is created to be united to her divine Spouse, the bridegroom who dreamed of her before time began and who longs to be united with her in heaven at the greatest wedding feast imaginable. On earth she can also be a bride, married to an earthly spouse whom she is meant to assist to heaven, or committed to her Heavenly One through consecrated life.

Here's the kicker: the task of preparing a daughter for marriage must begin early, earlier even than her dreams of it.

After giving a talk on this subject at a conference, I was approached by a devout Catholic mother who was a decade into the situation of having to raise two daughters without their father, who had left, in the home. She was passionate about her responsibility to pass along God's vision of true love to them.

She understood, thankfully, that this responsibility did not include bad-mouthing their father or even trying to fill his role herself. Rather, she put her energy into keeping the lines of communication with the girls open, raising them in the entire faith of the Church, and spending time around strong marriages so that her girls can see what it is they were ultimately made for, agape love and commitment.

That woman is a hero to me. She thanked me for giving a talk about raising girls. I thanked her for having the courage to embrace the task and not simply the talk.

I then thanked God for sending me a husband who, in spite of his aversion to musicals, is everything I could want in a spouse. Not only is he committed to our marriage, but he takes seriously his role in preparing our daughters for theirs.

.... *contemplation* ....

Do you know what your children's vision of marriage is? Do they want to be married, or do they at least see lifelong, committed marriage as a solid option for men and women who are called to it?

How does your marriage speak to your children of God's love for his Church, an image which it is intended to model? Do they see a life-giving love modeled in your marriage?

If you are no longer married, do you speak mean-spiritedly of your ex-spouse in your children's presence? Do you admit to mistakes you may have made in the marriage and have you sought reconciliation where it may be found? Do you still speak to your children of marriage as God's plan for the family?

······································ *action* ·····································

For married parents: Read 1 Corinthians 13:4-7 and write down the following eleven phrases in your journal, one on very other line: patient, kind, not jealous, not pompous, not inflated, not rude, not self-seeking, not quick tempered, not brooding, does not rejoice in the other's wrongdoing, rejoices in the truth. Next to each phrase, write a time when your marriage fulfilled this phrase; for example, write down a time when you were patient next to the word patient, a time when you were kind next to the word kind, etc. If you cannot think of an example for one, leave it blank and focus on doing something (or not doing something as the case may be) that will fulfill that particular aspect of St. Paul's definition.

Find a nearby course on John Paul II's work *Theology of the Body* and attend it with your spouse. Many courses and books on the subject offer ways to bring the ideas of self-donation and spousal love into your everyday language with your child. Katrina Zeno's books and seminars are offered nationwide, for every age and vocation and are a brilliant resource for this information. (For more information, go to the Women of the Third Millennium website at http://wttm.org). The earlier you begin with your child on the lessons contained in these eye-opening teachings, the better preparation you are giving them for whatever vocation to which they are called. However, as my husband and I were told from a 74 year-old friend who recently participated in a Theology of the Body seminar, "you are never too old to find out how you are supposed to love people."

For parents who are no longer married: Discuss marriage with your child honestly. Ask them if they have considered marriage for themselves as a vocation, and what they expect that marriage to look like. Ask them to be totally honest with you about where their ideas come from. Read the verses of Paul's first Letter to the Corinthians mentioned above together, and talk about what each of those means to your child. Consider that this is not a description of some ideal, unachievable love, but a very tangible and possible love between true friends and between spouses. Try to come up together with examples of marriages and relationships where you have seen these qualities demonstrated.

THE FRUITS *of a advent heart*

During more than one Advent season I have had the great joy of being pregnant right along with our Blessed Mother, sharing a period of waiting with Mary who "Mary kept all these things, pondering them in her heart." (Luke 2:19)

Our heart should be like a womb during Advent. Mary's was. She had God's promise in her heart, fed by little moments of revelation: An angel. Her cousin John dancing in his mother's womb. A child stirring within her own womb, each month even more, the Savior's kicks.

And then of course, there were those shepherds that came to meet her son soon after his birth.

This last revelation is worth meditating upon. After giving birth in less than sanitary conditions Mary welcomed strangers into her circumstances. They probably stayed a while as she struggled to comfort and nurse her newborn child. It is likely they could not take their eyes off of the Savior, the promise of two thousand years. And there she was, just having given birth, showing her son to visitors.

I can imagine the moment went something like this…

Joseph: Dear, I am sorry to bother you. How is he doing? Is he eating yet? There are some shepherds here that have come to see Jesus. They say that angels came to them in the fields and told them about…

Mary: *Angels???*

She knew about such couriers and her heart filled with joy that she and her husband were not alone in God's provision of heralds.

Mary: *Send them in!*

Perhaps she propped herself up on her elbow and showed them the sleeping child. And her eyes filled with tears when they beheld him with such awe and wonder. Perhaps she had wondered until then if she and her family were alone in the truth, the miracle of this promised and perfect little boy. But God had revealed his plan to others who saw the great worth of her small child.

"Is this him?" they might have asked in accord. "Is this the Savior of Israel?"

"Yes," she whispered. And the tears she could not hold back, those filled with the knowledge she had "held in her heart" for nine months, poured forth like water behind a broken dam.

"This is him," she sobbed with humble gratitude.

Each Advent we have the chance to hold all the knowledge of Christ's coming in our hearts: the words of Isaiah, the Psalms, the Gospels; to let that knowledge grow and move like a child in the womb. Like a pregnant mother, we become a sign to others, full of his promise of life, so full that our regular trappings don't fit, and we must change them. Everything about our earthly garments, our visible shell, begins to change and reflect the Lord's goodness.

And after moments in the presence of this joy, strangers can't help but ask, *Is that Him?* And we answer, *Yes,* glad that they too have seen His goodness.

Then perhaps those strangers can reflect God's presence to others, like water reflects the sky. And they do it not because they saw a tree in a store or heard someone say "Merry Christmas" instead of "Happy Holidays," but because they experienced his presence and shared it with others.

Then perhaps the words of Isaiah will take on flesh again: "a little child shall lead them... for the earth shall be full of the knowledge of the LORD as the waters cover the sea." (Isaiah 11: 6,9).

What was your family's Advent like last year? Is it even memorable? Did you celebrate Advent or was your focus on the trappings of a more commercial Christmas? Did your family feel closer to Christ and to one another by Christmas than they did at the start of Advent?

What is one change you would like to make this Advent in order to bring your family closer in faith to one another?

action

This Advent, commit to readings from Scripture each day. The daily readings of the Mass are selected so carefully during Advent that it is nearly impossible not to be closer to Christ by Christmas than you would have been without them. The USCCB website has the daily readings and they are able to be printed out easily. A subscription to Magnificat magazine, which contains the daily readings throughout the year, is also a good option. Reading all of the daily readings as a family would be ideal, but even focusing on just the Old Testament Readings during the week and then all of the readings before Mass on Sunday would create a scriptural focus for your family. In the later evening when homework and extracurricular activities are finished, is a great time to gather as a family around an Advent wreath during the week.

Bring these readings into every day life in little ways. Perhaps taking a simple excerpt from the previous day's reading – maybe something that stood out to your child during the reading – and writing it on a note card tucked into a lunchbox can be the simple reminder to your child of Advent during her week. (Note that such reminders need not be for just Advent. Even a simple note that says, "I am praying for your test today" or "Never forget how much you are loved" could brighten a tween's bad day and remind them that home is where they can feel close to Christ.)

During this same Advent period, begin recording in your journal changes you see in yourself and your family during Advent.

BRING ON THE *holy family at advent*

I know there are those who really poo-poo the idea of stores starting their Christmas marketing in early November. Not this mom. For me, it is a welcome change from the ghoulish figures of Halloween that began filling the minds of my children in August.

By November the nightmares created by some ridiculous headless goblin with a gruesome laugh give way to images of joy and cheer: a cultured snowman with a top hat and cane, a busy bearded fellow in red who is still happily married to his concerned and involved wife of too many years to count, lots of dutiful little workers who believe, as their boss does, that the most important people on earth – children – are never seen as a burden.

Some would say I am overstating the value of secular Christmas images. Perhaps I am. In our house, however, all those images stand willingly in the shadow of the greatest image of the season: the Holy Family.

For two months out of the year our family is surrounded by images of the Holy Family. It's my own fault since I collect them. Our home is filled with nativities, mother-and-child figurines, and multi-medium fashionings of the three people I most admire: Jesus, Mary, and Joseph.

Like other families, one of our many Christmas traditions is to have our family portrait taken for Christmas cards. I am always impressed if the photographer gets most of us looking at the camera, never mind looking holy.

In my son's eye is usually a twinkle of mischief, his older sister seems to be posing for a little princess competition, and our youngest has the look of any child who is being cajoled by a squeaky toy on the other side of the camera. My husband looks handsome and strong, and I often look a touch better than tired.

As the cards from friends and family pour in to our mailbox in increasing number each year, we begin another of our traditions: our Holy Family prayer wall. Each family's picture is attached to a garland made by the little hands in our house. As we fix them in place, one by one, we say the simple prayer, "Jesus, make them a holy family." When the season is over, those photos will be cut and placed into a scrap book for each of our children so they can pray for the families throughout the year. The fighting over each picture is less than holy, but the end result, we hope, is sanctifying for someone.

The bottom line is that we are teaching our children that images mean something.

The image of the family is one we want burned into their little minds as holy. It's the reason we teach them to write "JMJ" at the top of their school papers. It's the reason that each of our kids has his or her own miniature nativity set. Because enough time spent sitting in front of those precious figures will fix an image in their mind. And no matter how you move them around, those little figures only make sense when their gaze is fixed on Christ.

Ergo, they'll conclude, when Jesus is the center of the family, then any family can be holy.

·· *contemplation* ··

What images come to mind when you think of Christmas? Are they mostly holy, secular or a mix?

What images fill your home during the Christmas season? Are they mostly secular, mostly religious, or a mix? How does this display affect your child's imagination and how does it form in their minds the importance, or lack of, holy images during Christmas?

·· *action* ··

This year during Advent, choose to change one secular thing in your family's approach to Christmas tradition, such as adding a scriptural phrase instead of "Happy Holidays" on your Christmas cards, or making a gingerbread Nativity Set instead of a plain gingerbread house with the children. Give as gifts little images of the Holy Family instead of regular ornaments. In our home where we teach that the saints are always turning our focus to Christ, St. Nicholas brings gifts for each child in their stocking that remind them of the true meaning of the season. Read with your children Lori Walburg VandenBosch's *The Legend of the Candy Cane*, a tale that teaches Christian imagery attached to the holiday's most popular confection, and attach a summary of it to candy canes for your neighbors or friends as gifts.

One Advent, listen with your family to Handel's Messiah, preferably at a live concert. Focus particularly on Part 1 which contains Scripture's prophesies of the coming Messiah to the angels who visited the shepherds after His birth. The Old and New Testament accounts of the events are sung in such a way that they make an indelible impression on the human imagination not unlike that of a holy image. After listening, discuss as a family over dessert the following statement by Handel when he was approached after the first London performance of *Messiah* by an aristocrat who hailed his ability to "entertain" listeners with it. Handel replied, *"My Lord, I should be sorry if I only entertain them; I wish to make them better."*

CREATING A SIMPLE ATMOSPHERE
for Christ at advent

The headlines of November 2008 read that Christmas sales would be at an all time low due to an economic recession. Add to that an increasing number of families struggling with unemployment and loss of income, and by any child's standard the vision of a tree towering over lots of gifts was pretty bleak. In general, it appeared to be shaping up as a pretty dismal Christmas. And yet, there existed that year an opportunity for the most wonderful Christmas since Tiny Tim said grace with Ebenezer Scrooge.

Taking advantage of the corresponding housing market in a down economy, my husband and I did what we swore only three years prior to never do again: move. Apparently suffering from a short-term amnesia regarding the details involved with packing a home, we decided to relocate closer to church and family.

In addition to being nearer to those we love, our decision yielded another benefit which I discovered on moving day: my growing detachment to our excessive belongings. As the contents of our house rolled away in a jam-packed 26-foot moving truck, I honestly thought that, barring any injury to the drivers, I wouldn't have minded if that two-ton trinket-toting trailer of my material life was blown to smithereens.

Granted, I was tired of the boxes and packing tape, but even more, I was taken aback by how much we had accumulated over time. One week of living out of boxes quickly taught me how very little we really need, and the overlapping season of Advent during that move could not have been more perfect for such a revelation.

Our Christmas that year, due in part to maintenance expenditures on the older home we had bought, was simple. In fact, Advent itself began with far less extravagance than I usually afford it with my collection of nativity sets and related tchotchkes. Having been unable to locate the appropriate boxes of seasonal decorations in time, our family was left with only one option for celebrating the first week of Advent: a walk down to church where the décor and message of the season are simple, and quite different from the grocery store across the street.

Our two older children immediately ran to the parish "giving tree," filled with tags requesting far less stuff than would fill a 26-foot truck. Personal hygiene items, and other small things that might help someone less fortunate maintain their dignity this winter, were the focus of our children's little hearts, so hungry for the season's meaning. They concluded, in this simple atmosphere, that if the meaning of Christmas is God's greatest gift of His Son, then the least we could do was give of ourselves to others.

On our walk home, tags in hand, we decided that in addition to buying the small items requested, we would pray for Christ to become present to each of the persons receiving the items. We also decided that He needed to become as present in our own home as He was in our hearts at that moment. So boxes were cleared away from atop the kitchen table and in their stead was placed our Advent wreath. Next to that – after locating it during a mad search and rescue in our crowded garage – we placed our favorite set of little nativity figures, all staring at an empty manger and longing, like we are, for God to save us from our tendency to forget what is most important and show us again the greatest gift to which all others pale by comparison.

contemplation

When you think of Christmas décor, what images come to mind?

Is your home dressed in such a way that the atmosphere lends itself to a more reverent holiday for you and your family than the department store?

This Advent, consider making one small item, like an Advent wreath or nativity set, the center of your seasonal décor. Place it somewhere prominent and make that spot the gathering place for evening prayer and Advent readings for your family. Have everyone participate in the reading and prayer, or rotate the leader each night. During the last week of Advent, have the family share this different approach to the season, and share what they liked and didn't like about it.

Consider changing your Christmas traditions entirely one year. We know a family that tried the following changes one year and has never gone back since. This family does not put out the tree until Christmas Eve, and they do not begin decorating it until Christmas morning. For the next twelve days, they each add one decoration to the tree and then on the Feast of the Epiphany, they finally open gifts, recalling those brought by the Magi to Christ in the manger. Christmas morning is also spent doing a service project as a family, like delivering food boxes or gifts to needy children. Their children say it is their favorite time of year and exactly the way they want to celebrate the holidays with their families when they grow up.

part 4

WHERE IS MY HONORARY DEGREE?

RAISING *a princess*

I am a Target mom – a Target audience you might say. Moms are Target audiences. I can go into that store with a very specific list of three things that I need, and in eight minutes I have so deviated from my list that I find myself justifying a chenille throw pillow for the guest room I do not have because it is a bargain forty percent off. I know similar moms – we are part of a support group. (I think there are similar groups for men who shop at The Apple Store and Home Depot, but you may want to check your local listings on this.)

So when I saw Target giving in to a popular Princess motif which had wooed so many other whiny young girls into being not princesses, but spoiled children, I was of course concerned. I would *not* be a victim, and neither would my daughter.

Too often I had seen little girls with tiaras and lip gloss who couldn't be six years old, insisting that the newest princess Barbie be theirs. Target knows this, by the way, which is why they plant the Barbie princess in such a location as to trip moms who are otherwise focused like a laser beam on their three-item list.

I had two options: stop shopping at Target, or turn this princess thing into a theme I could use for the Kingdom. Alas, Target *did* comply with the request of shoppers like myself who demanded they end their support of Planned Parenthood in order to retain our patronage, so it turned out I had only one option.

The princess theme, unfortunately, was not the end of what I was beginning to see as a pattern of self-aggrandizing messages attempting to teach little girls their worth by comparison to boys (who are "dumb" according to one shirt) or other girls (who are not "spoiled rotten" as another touted).

It wasn't long before my daughter wanted a Princess birthday party like her friends, and a Princess costume for Halloween, and costumes to spare for playing dress up. While it is easy enough to explain as I have before that "we don't always get what we want" and we "should count all the blessings we *do* have" I felt that these desires in particular merited special attention.

And so my husband and I prayed about it, and soon began to teach our daughter the truth about her royalty. We told her that she *is* a princess because her Daddy is the King of Kings, and that the riches to be gained from that identity are immeasurable, especially here on Earth. Even Scripture tells us that royal dignity has been ours since the day of our birth (Ps 110:3).

So she had a Princess birthday party, but with a slightly different angle. Her invitation was a little poem that read,

I am a little princess, My daddy the King of Kings,
He lavishes me with kindness and riches more than rings,
Like Grace and Mercy boundless and a love so strong it sings.
I am a little princess, My daddy the King of Kings

With patience He's shown favor when lesser dads would quit,
Such times I fear to reckon how this tarnished crown would fit,
But my Daddy goes before me so it's to his robe I cling,
I am His little princess and He the King of Kings.

It was a grand success and we all suffered for days from pink-frosted hangovers.

After attending a Catholic Women's Conference that same month, in which the theme was similar to the poem above, I was reminded of just how many women had not heard this message about their inherent dignity. Without that knowledge, these women admitted to searching elsewhere for affirmation and in short, like the country song suggests, looked for love "in all the wrong places." So I was glad we had taken a proactive approach with our daughters in getting the message through to them.

It wasn't much later that I saw the fruits of our effort. While I was out with my then-five year old daughter one day, we saw a little girl wearing a sparkly tiara. Smiling, my daughter asked her if she was a princess. The little girl responded with a rather annoyed "Yeah" that might as well have been a "Duh," as if it were self-explanatory. Thrilled, my daughter began jumping up and down, and shouted, "Mom! Mom! Her Daddy's Jesus too!"

contemplation

When you have conversations with your daughter about her friends and her life, how does she speak about herself and others? Does she use language that demonstrates an understanding of her inherent dignity and the resulting respect that dignity should provoke? Or does her language suggest her self-worth and those of her friends is based on the shifting opinion of others? What does her dress and her attitude around others suggest to you about this? Does she seem to understand that women who have Christ as the source of their self-worth can transform the world, or does she see this vision of women as powerless?

action

A wonderful organization dedicated to instilling women of all ages with reassurance and reminders of their dignity is ENDOW (which stands for Educating on the Nature and Dignity of Women). Visit www.endowonline.com and find out more about their courses and events offered to women. Many of the courses are downloadable and while much of the material is geared toward women of all ages, they also have resources geared specifically toward teen girls. You can review them with your daughter and also find links to ENDOW courses being offered in your area. This is a wonderful opportunity for a mother and daughter to share, but fathers should not shy away from facilitating this opportunity for their daughters as well. Since ENDOW has put the courses and literature together for you, much time is saved in trying to find the right resources that will teach your daughter the Catholic view of her self-worth in Christ.

THE GRACE *of parental humility*

I have to believe that the number one thing that keeps most parents from being the light that God wants them to be to their children is Pride, followed by a close second in Selfishness. On more instances than I can count, I have seen God use my children to humble me. And yet, the stubborn part of me that still tries to live for myself is compelled to control the least controllable situation. I have actually, during my toddler's department store tantrum, found myself thinking that if only I had read one more parenting book, I could handle the situation properly.

On the first Sunday of Lent one year, my husband and I brought our two young children who were recovering from a two-week long cold with us into Mass. Before entering the sanctuary, I explained to them they were to be on their best behavior, as always, in the Lord's house.

But my two angels had apparently contracted with one another in the back seat of the van, as only brilliant toddlers can do, their modus operandi of mischief during service. In a miraculous rebound from their once sedative infirmity, they had been taken over by new energy and by what would appear to be amnesia regarding church etiquette. Witnessing them, I had to believe that more than one bystander speculated the two had been locked in a crate for the last five hours and fed sugar cubes.

There I was, in all my pride, frustrated with both my children's behavior and my parenting skills, and deflecting God's abundant grace in the Mass like I had Wonder Woman's wristbands on. And there I was, choking on the smoke of my lamp, lit only minutes prior, now under a bushel basket, with a big fat ego sitting on top.

Just then, when I was about to reach boiling point, counting all the opportunities for grace my husband and I were missing by paying these two strange children our constant and draining attention, I heard it.

From the choir came the words, *"Be still and know that He is God."*

The words lifted my head. And there He was, hanging on the cross for this moment when I might choose to think that I am failing as a parent, that it is really all up to me to get this right. And I recalled that something else, greater than my pride, is unremitting, too: His abundant grace.

In that moment of recalling my Savior's agony on the cross I was humbled, and my eyes were opened to see the sympathetic smile of a mom standing next to her three teenagers one row over. I know that smile well. I gave it to a mother with young ones the week before when my kids were behaving themselves and hers had eaten sugar cubes.

So it came down to community, to sacrifice, and to no surprise, dying to myself, in order to find the Lord I hadn't realized I had lost sight of. At that moment, in my once-ironed dress now wrinkled and covered with the remnants of my child's fleeting head cold, I felt closer to Jesus than before.

Out of ideas, out of myself, He brought me closer and lit my lamp again. Then loud and clear were the words "Go *in peace* to love and serve the Lord."

Yes, this is where my peace comes from. *Thanks be to God.*

contemplation

When was the last time you were humbled in public by your child's actions? What was the result of that humiliation? Did you turn inside yourself, or did you turn to Christ?

When a friend shares a moment of her own like this with you, do you remind her that her strength as a parent is found in Christ, or do you frustrate her by complaining about parenthood?

action

If you struggle with not being able to control your child's every move, take this cross to the Lord and offer it up. Make this your focus in prayer for one week. Journal about it. Eventually God may reveal this source of frustration as a manifestation of Pride or of a lack of trust in Him.

Write down the following words on a note card and keep it in a place where you pray often: *God chose you out of all of eternity to be the parent of this particular child, and He knew what He was doing. He made you and designed you not to be perfect, but to be the perfect parent for this particular child. Parenting on earth is only shepherding. Your child's real parent is God the Father, and He will give you the strength and the humility to lead this child home to Heaven. Just ask Him, and trust Him.*

Ask the Blessed Mother, the one whom God chose to be the Mother of his Son, to pray for you. If you aren't doing so already, being saying a regular Rosary. As you meditate on the mysteries of Christ's life, ask God to give you humility like Mary so you can be the shepherd He wants you to be.

Read a biography of the life of St. Monica, the mother of St. Augustine. Though Augustine is now considered a Doctor of the Church, there were many years (alluded to in his *Confessions*) when he was far from God and living a life of sin. His mother prayed fervently and never gave up on him. Augustine's eventual conversion to the faith is often credited to her unwavering intercession for him while on earth. When you are struggling with your child's behavior, ask St. Monica to pray for you the way only she can.

FINDING *a role model*

In the summer preceding my junior year in high school, I attended a John Macleod basketball camp held at Northern Arizona University in Flagstaff. In addition to a week away from my parents and camaraderie with team members, I was most looking forward to meeting my NBA idol: the architect of the two-handed, behind-the-back slam dunk, Larry Nance. I had even saved up for a slick new pair of high-tops just so I could get his autograph on them.

The morning of his presentation, I wriggled my way up to the front of a hundred high schoolers in the Lumberjack gym – clasping tightly my unworn pair of Nikes - and awaited his pearls of wisdom on life and sports and that famous slam dunk. Disappointment does not begin to describe my reaction to not only the lack of pearls, but to his refusal afterwards to sign my shiny white shoes. I was heartbroken.

The next day we gathered again before drills, this time to hear motivation from some lesser known NBA player with a Slavic last name I couldn't pronounce. He spoke to us about the importance of practice, perseverance, and the potential of every person for excellence. Then he attempted to make a basket from every angle of the 3-point perimeter *twice* in under three minutes, starting again from the beginning if he missed any shot. He did it, in just under three minutes. It was more than impressive to my sixteen year old eyes – it was inspiring - and I let him sign my shoes.

Many of us recall the notorious commercial starring NBA star Charles Barkley who proudly opened with the words "I am not a role model." It came at a time when sports stars' lives were beginning to dupe their fans who thought them to be pretty upstanding citizens. Barkley's words, though initially controversial, became the proud slogan of many who found themselves relieved of the task of having to live a life above reproach. Somehow "role model" had been mistaken for "super hero," and knowing the later didn't actually exist led us all to conclude the former was also impossible.

Any parent knows better. Parents know that their job necessarily entails modeling behavior. And a paparazzi-shadowed lifestyle ain't got nothin' on a stay-at-home parent's, which is constantly lived in front of children's eyes. This is where I find the wisdom of that then-lesser known basketball player so important. A life lived above reproach is impossible without practice, persistence and the knowledge that each of us can work toward excellence. These principles translate for Christians as regular prayer, reliance on grace, and the reminder that we are each made in God's image.

When in doubt of role models, consider St. Augustine of Hippo. A man fraught with pride and licentiousness, he concluded in his autobiographical *Confessions* a certain truth which gives Barkley's motto a run for the role model's money: "We are restless until we rest in God." Restlessness is not the goal, but the inspiration. In our restlessness, we must seek God's will, knowing it is to him that we are ultimately modeling our behavior. For parents, children are simply the immediate litmus test of its quality.

I still have my McLeod Camp high-tops, signed by my role model at age sixteen, NBA All-star Jeff Hornacek. They are completely worn from countless basketball drills and discipline that lead to games won and lost. I have taken them out on a tough day of parenting, or when I hear my own words come from my children's mouths and they are less than exemplary. They lead me to solicit prayer from my other role models, the Saints, and then I thank God for the opportunity and the reasons in parenthood to aspire toward holiness.

·· *contemplation* ··

Who are your role models in regard to parenting and married life? What about your professional life? Why?

Do you know who your child's role models are?

Is your behavior, your profession, your marriage, something that your child admires and may even want to imitate?

The next time you are out with your child, ask him who some of his role models are, and ask him to explain why he chose them. Ask about the role models of their friends if they know.

Pray that God would make you a worthy role model for your child in the different aspects of your life: marriage, parenthood, professional life. Ask Him to change you where necessary and give you the strength to be true to this privilege of being a parent whose actions are examples.

The church's saints are inspiring role models. There is virtually a saint for every profession, vocation and lifestyle. Buy a book of saints for your child and give it to them as a gift. If there is a particular saint they are fond of, mark the page with a note card that has an inspiring quote written on it like Mother Teresa's "Be faithful in small things because it is in them that your strength lies."

LEAVEN HELP US:
the gift of the domestic church

If you are one of those people convinced that contemporary American families are turning out a generation to whom the idea of hard work is as far afield from their daily fare as Latin lessons, then you haven't met the Usher boys.

I'll admit when I received notice that the oldest three of the eight Usher children were looking for a way to make some money to attend a Catholic boys' camp this summer, I was feeling both generous if a little pessimistic. But because I believe in helping kids earn money for such things, I told their mom they could pull our weeds and mow our lawn for what I thought was a generous amount of money, even, I thought, if they did only a half-decent job.

Three and a half hours after their arrival, as the boys continued to slave away leaving no weed unpulled, no blade of grass too long, and not one of our outdoor toys strewn about, I began to panic. Their attention to detail and work ethic were deserving of far more than I had originally contracted with their mother, and yet I didn't have enough to pay them more.

I called a mutual friend who was of little help. She explained to me that what I was witnessing was "just the Usher family," and went on to illustrate other occasions where they had done similar things, like unpacking the moving truck of a new family in the area and refuse to take any money for it. I soon understood that were it not for their summer camp goal, these boys would have chalked those hours in the unforgiving sun over my yard to charity. They just seemed to appreciate the opportunity to serve.

What also interested me was that the boys' father was as hard at work on our lawn as they were. Of course he was their ride, the boys being too young to drive, but he did not act as a foreman. Rather, he was a first-hand teacher of servanthood. In essence, he was a model of Jesus' earthly father. Though I have never met St. Joseph, I have an idea that Jesus' attention to detail and work ethic were things he learned from his carpenter father.

My children pressed their faces up against the window in awe of the whole thing: four young boys (another son had come along just to be helpful) and their father, working -without breaks - to make our yard look like the cover of a home and garden magazine.

It was more than my six year old could take. She filled our finest glass pitcher with ice water and slices of citrus, and asked if she could serve them. When her emptied pitcher didn't seem like enough, she and her brother created small works of art as thank you's for this family who had labored harder than my kids could imagine trying to themselves. After they left, my daughter asked me if their oldest was going to be a priest.

And thus the lesson of "the domestic church" and its role in salvation was complete. And my lawn was stunning. Through this exchange between two families, we witnessed firsthand that when actions are rooted in love, they do not end in themselves, but are life-giving. In this way the family is leaven to a world in need of hope.

So to anyone who may feel uncertain of the church's future I give you the reason for my hope, evidence of what John Paul II called "a new springtime of Christianity:" it's families like the Ushers.

Those who serve in love are witnesses of the faith. Their charity bears fruit, leading others to the source of their joy which is Christ. In short, as Pope Benedict XVI said on his 2008 visit to the United States, such people "point the way toward that vast horizon of hope that God is even now opening up to His Church, and indeed to all humanity: the vision of a world reconciled and renewed in Christ Jesus, our Savior."

When was the last time your entire family did service work together? What was the result of that service in regard to the family's cohesion and attitude toward one another?

Discuss with your child a fond memory they have of helping someone. Ask them to help you come up with a service project in which the entire family can be involved in helping others.

One of the most common reasons that people give for losing their faith is the actions of "so-called Christians" which seem to be unloving. Though this may be an excuse, you can still be the contrary example to this theory. Begin with serving those in your own extended family if you live near them. If you have family members who are far from God or have left their Catholic faith, begin with them in service. Visit this family member more often, and help them where they have practical needs like yard or housework, meals, academic help, etc.

Remind your family members of two things: our actions reflect our relationship (or lack of) with Christ (John 13:35) and service done in love bears fruit and gives glory to God.

If you don't do it already, pray before meals as a family when you are out in public. This simple thing can make quite an impact on those around you.

Sit as a family toward the front of church the next time you are at Mass. Not only will it be easier for your family to pay attention to what is going on, but you will be one less family encouraging others to crowd the back of church.

RAISING *pro-life kids*

Growing up in my house must have seemed pretty strange to friends who visited. Rather than the shopping mall, our family outings often involved trips to soup kitchens, nursing homes, and the home of a single mother of seven in South Phoenix with two sons in prison. Our spare room was more than once home to a very pleasant nomadic gentleman named Harry who occasionally drifted into town looking for work and a place to stay. And nary a Christmas passed that my father didn't invite some displaced soul to share in our abundant table and to unwrap a small gift he had bought just in case we had a visitor.

I still recall a friend who thought the only thing stranger than my not having MTV was that I was part of a regular seniors card game at Scottsdale Heritage Court and knew each person there by name. To me, these things didn't seem strange at all; just a normal part of growing up in my parents' house.

At the age of seventeen, I experienced a defining moment in my "pro-life formation." On Christmas morning, my dad took my brothers and me to a house of hospitality dedicated to serving the poor and homeless in Phoenix, to distribute food boxes.

Fifteen minutes into our first run, a homeless and handicapped veteran on the corner screamed into my window, "Hey, Lady! You got a couple dollars?!?!" My dad reached over my trembling body, gave the man a meal voucher and a firm handshake, and drove away saying, "See, Honey, down here you get called a *lady.*"

It was not until I became a parent myself that I reflected upon this moment and realized that the task of raising pro-life children isn't so much about participating in isolated pro-life events as it is living out as best one can the model of Christ.

Raising pro-life kids, then, is really as simple as fostering a climate that edifies life, and it looks something like this: celebrating and supporting large families; dropping off baby supplies to a home for pregnant women; letting children see the life-giving love of a marriage lived with Natural Family Planning; and volunteering as a family in a soup kitchen or a nursing home.

Being a pro-life family is about more than just financially supporting pro-life organizations, though this is certainly necessary and important; it's about spending time with those lives they support. In doing so, we teach our children to do more than defend life; we show them what life is, precious in every form and always full of dignity.

As a result, and quite naturally part of God's plan, our children will become respecters of life, however countercultural. And consequently, they will rally to defend life just as they would a younger brother who is being picked on. Their Catholic faith, so life-affirming, will then become a natural extension of who they are.

Because contrary to popular bumper sticker philosophy, goodness is not found in the practice of random acts of kindness. It is found in the deliberate and consistent service of life at every stage. This surely defines for children what it means to be God's creation, and indeed what it means to be a Christian.

.... *contemplation* ....

What is your family's general attitude about larger families? What do you consider a "large" family? Do you know many families with more than three children? Do you spend time with them?

When your child spends time with an elderly person, how does he behave? Is he uncomfortable? Is it such a rare occasion that he doesn't know what to say or how to behave? Do you model behavior around the elderly which shows your child that they are full of dignity and to be treated with respect?

Do any of the following life-affirming projects as a family in your community:

Help a local shut-in or handicapped neighbor with yard work or a run to the grocery store.

Collect baby items for a local women's shelter.

If you have young children, have them make cards for residents in a nursing home and call the nursing home to set up a visit. Ask the director to show you the person(s) in the home who rarely get visitors and begin there with your visit. That visit may take up your whole afternoon since those people might be starving for conversation and companionship.

Depending on how the project goes, consider continuing it on a regular basis.

HAPPY CAMPERS:
the life lessons and heavenly times of family trips

I imagine most of us have had tent experiences. Maybe it was the blanket-draped-over the-dining-room-chairs variety or the backyard canvas fort set-up with thirty neighborhood kids going in and out until all fell down. Then there was the first real overnight at a campground trying to sleep on bumpy, uneven earth while siblings stepped on each other during a midnight trek to the latrine.

Whichever the case, each experience taught us a little something about the inimitable role of family. My father, a civil engineer, was our hero the way he could make a duffel bag full of seemingly mismatched poles, ropes, canvases and ground stakes become a livable shelter for our family of six.

My brothers and I were shaped by a hundred experiences out in the wild, from mastering the proper composition of the aforementioned duffle bag contents, to the physics of creek stone skipping, to the art of marshmallow charring, to discovering the immeasurable value of applying mosquito repellent before sundown.

One camping lesson even included an experiment with planting popcorn! When our unfastened car-top carrier blew its lid during a rushed ride to a small town church, the local prairie was covered with the contents of a three-foot long bag of yellow, salted kid-sustenance. I never researched it, but I'll bet Verde Valley grew an unexpected crop of corn the next year.

There is something about having nothing to do for days but hunt for sticks, hike, fish, and play card games with the same people which bonds family in a way that choreographed nights around the TV simply can't.

I can remember thinking that Heaven would smell like campfires and wet pine trees. Besides, didn't Peter at one point ask Jesus – in the presence of two heaven-dwelling figures - if they could pitch three tents? I knew there would be camping in Heaven!

At some point in my late adolescence our family graduated to a tent camper on wheels that we owned in partnership with another family. What luxury! Then we were off to neighboring states and rendezvousing with cousins who were traveling cross country in similar digs.

Luxurious a dwelling as it was, cranking up our house and zipping up our windows at night did a lot to help us appreciate the real thing when we got home. So did six people asleep in a space the size of a small kitchen, sink and all. Home looked extra sweet to us after many such trips.

And it was at home, in the off season, when our camper found new uses. Parked on the side of our house, that happy little beast made sleepovers with friends fulfilling to a juvenile's sense of adventure and seclusion, while still being only a stone's throw from the amenities that one often misses on a camping trip; namely, a stocked fridge and an ample bathroom.

Once it even served as home to a local 20 year old who had no place to stay. My folks let him make our trailer his abode for about six weeks, coming into the house through the back door for some of the necessities of life. I am pretty sure my dad changed out the camper's "wall art" often during his stay, alternating various and encouraging scripture passages on colored note cards. I pray he was helped. At least he surely learned what we learned from both tent and camper: a home can be a home, be it ever so humble.

When we are forced by economic conditions to live with less, let us remember that to be "wholly" family does not require more stuff and busier schedules to offset what we lack at home. It does require an environment which fosters love for those whom God has given us to care for.

When was the last time you took a simple vacation as just a family? Do you have fond memories of taking family trips as a child? Does this affect how often you create opportunities for such trips in your family today?

If you haven't ever been camping, how does the idea strike you? Does it seem like a simple and fun vacation, or stressful and lacking too many comforts?

action

Take a camping trip as a family. If you do not have equipment, borrow it. If you have never been camping and the idea overwhelms you, begin with a "campout" in the back yard with all the fixins: tent, sleeping bags, marshmallows, flashlights. No television, no cell phones, no portable games.

When you go on the next family trip, be sure to include two things in your itinerary: prayer and games. Bring along a deck of cards and everyone's favorite junk food for a "game night." Have contests on who can tell the best story, or put together the "Family Story Memory Awards" in which the winner of Funniest Family Moment Story, Most Embarrassing Story, Happiest Time in Our Family Story, etc wins a handmade award created earlier in the day from simple, silly supplies.

On the way home from any trip, we always play "What's Your Favorite" with our children. Our aim is to find what part of the trip was the highlight for them. We are always surprised at their answers, which completely vary based on their love language and personality, and the knowledge helps us to plan the next trip even better.